Pub. 10.00

Twayne's English Authors Series

EDITOR OF THIS VOLUME

Sarah W. R. Smith

Tufts University

Robert Bloomfield

TEAS 310

Robert Bloomfield

ROBERT BLOOMFIELD

By JONATHAN LAWSON

Saint Cloud State University

TWAYNE PUBLISHERS
A DIVISION OF G. K. HALL & CO., BOSTON

Copyright © 1980 by G. K. Hall & Co.

Published in 1980 by Twayne Publishers,
A Division of G. K. Hall & Co.
All Rights Reserved

Printed on permanent/durable acid-free paper and bound
in the United States of America

First Printing

Library of Congress Cataloging in Publication Data

Lawson, Jonathan.
Robert Bloomfield.

(Twayne's English authors series ; TEAS 310)
Bibliography: pp. 163–68
Includes index.
1. Bloomfield, Robert, 1766–1823.   2. Poets,
English—19th century—Biography.
PR4149.B6Z75   821'.7 [B]   80-15696
ISBN 0-8057-6802-5

For J. W. C.

Contents

About the Author

Jonathan N. Lawson is associate dean of Liberal Arts and Sciences and professor of English at St. Cloud State University, St. Cloud, Minnesota. He took his Ph.D. at Texas Christian University, specializing in eighteenth-century British literature. In 1969 he was awarded a TCU Research Foundation Grant to study the Bloomfield materials at the British Library. And in 1971, after accepting a position at St. Cloud, he completed *Collected Poems (1800–1822) by Robert Bloomfield,* a five-volume-in-one facsimile edition. In 1972, he again worked with Bloomfield materials in England and consulted with interested scholars there: the research was sponsored by the Minnesota State University Faculty Research Fund.

Professor Lawson, who directed the composition program at St. Cloud State University from 1972–77, is the author of reviews and articles on composition and rhetoric and the associate editor of the *Rhetoric Society of America Quarterly.* In 1974 he became executive secretary of Lambda Iota Tau, International Honor Society in Literature. At present Lawson is an American Council on Education Fellow in Academic Administration.

Preface

Robert Bloomfield was a farmer's boy, a shoemaker, and a surprisingly good rural poet. His skill in capturing the essence of rural life, its traditions, people, and landscape, is unmatched. With sensitivity and sympathy he described country life in Suffolk at the close of the eighteenth century, and for his labors he became briefly the rage of London.

The popularity which once elevated Bloomfield to a position of great potential influence is gone. When he died in 1823, only limited public notice marked his passing. Within one hundred years Bloomfield's name had been relegated to the footnotes of literary histories and his poems nearly forgotten. His verse has not, until recently, been easily available, and little more than passing reference is made to his career in contemporary studies of the romantic revival.

Bloomfield's fate may be all for the best. But as Edmund Blunden once lamented in "The Country Tradition," the amount of printed matter concerning the major figures and movements in literature has swollen beyond the point of usefulness while minor writers of genuine merit and virtue have been neglected.[1] Among that latter number, he asserted, is Robert Bloomfield whom we might be eulogizing or at least reading had England been less fertile in poets. Mr. Blunden may be correct, and readers who have a fondness for country traditions and a willingness to tolerate a rural poet's lapses may find in Bloomfield an appealing counterpoint to the major writers of his era.

This study has three general purposes. The first is to make available an adequate biographical portrait of the poet. Since most accounts of his life have been drawn from the preface to early editions of *The Farmer's Boy*, I have added here much information from Bloomfield's published and unpublished letters, from his manuscript notes penned in a copy of his first volume, and from sundry recent writings. Because it has been unavailable, I have set the biographical material in rather full form in simple chronological order.

The second aim is to examine Bloomfield's poetry, considering the few, scattered critical statements about him while presenting the first unified interpretation of his work. Although *The Farmer's Boy*, his most significant poem, is at the center of this study, I have attempted to discover the merits and weaknesses of seldom-mentioned later works. I have not dealt at any length with his prose and drama which are of less importance and merit. With a view of the man and his poetry in hand, the final objective is to note what literary, historical, and cultural importance Bloomfield's rural poetry might have.

My efforts were facilitated by grants from the Research Foundation at Texas Christian University and the Minnesota State University Faculty Research Fund which enabled me to read at the British Library and to explore the areas where Bloomfield lived. I am indebted to the librarians at the British Library, the Learning Resources Center at St. Cloud State University, and the Mary Couts Burnett Library at Texas Christian University for their assistance. Professor Jim W. Corder has my lasting gratitude for wise counsel and introducing me to Robert Bloomfield. To Professor Sarah W. R. Smith of Tufts University for her sensitive and sensible editing I owe special appreciation. Robert F. Ashby, F.L.A., Surrey County librarian, has my thanks for past kindness and encouragement.

Grateful acknowledgement is made to the following for permission to use quotations: The British Library for excerpts from Egerton MS 2245 and Additional MSS 26,265, 28,266, 28,268 and 30,809; Jacques Barzun and Harper & Row Publishers for excerpts from *Science, The Glorious Entertainment;* George Allen & Unwin Publishers for an excerpt from Rayner Unwin, *The Rural Muse;* and J. M. Dent & Sons, Ltd., for excerpts from *The Complete Works of William Hazlitt,* ed. P. P. Howe.

JONATHAN LAWSON

St. Cloud State University

Chronology

1766 Robert Bloomfield born December 3 at Honington in Suffolk to George and Elizabeth Bloomfield.

1767 Father dies of smallpox; mother supports six children by keeping the village school in her home.

1770 Goldsmith's *Deserted Village*.

1772 Sent for three months to Mr. Rodwell's school at Ixworth to be "improved in writing." Remarriage of his mother adds children to the crowded home.

ca. 1778 Becomes a "farmer's boy" for his mother's brother-in-law, William Austin of Sapiston on a farm in the manor of the duke of Grafton, later Bloomfield's patron.

1781 Journeys to London to live with his brother George and learn the trade of shoemaking.

1783 Crabbe's *The Village*.

ca. 1784 First attempts at verse. Lawful apprenticeship arranged.

1786 May, "The Village Girl" appears in Say's *Gazetteer*. Builds and sells aeolian harps.

1790 December 12, marries Mary Anne Church.

1791 October 25, Hannah, first child.

1796 May, composition of *The Farmer's Boy* begins.

1798 April, completion of *The Farmer's Boy*. September, *Lyrical Ballads* published by Wordsworth and Coleridge. Capel Lofft now a patron.

1800 *The Farmer's Boy*. Bloomfield soon a popular curiosity.

1801 Poems for the next edition completed; publication delayed by a feud between patron and publisher. Fifth edition of *The Farmer's Boy*.

1802 *Rural Tales, Ballads, and Songs*. Shoemaking still the steadiest source of income.

1803 Appointed undersealer in the King's Bench Court. Forced by his constitution to resign the post after only a few months. Death of his mother.

1804 The smallpox poem, *Good Tidings; or News From the Farm*. Readings for the Royal Jennerian Society.

1806 *Wild Flowers; or Pastoral and Local Poetry*.

1807 Tours the Wye.

1811 *The Banks of the Wye*. Hope for financial security shattered by the death of the Duke of Grafton and the failure of Bloomfield's bookseller.

1812 Quits London to find cheaper lodgings at Shefford in Bedfordshire. The popularity of his works declining.

1813 *The History of Little Davy's New Hat*, a children's book intended to teach rural values.

1816 Issue of a public subscription to aid the distressed poet.

1822 *May Day With the Muses*.

1823 *Hazelwood Hall; A Village Drama*. Bloomfield dies, impoverished, at Shefford on August 19.

1824 *The Remains of Robert Bloomfield* edited by Joseph Weston in an effort to aid the poet's family.

CHAPTER 1

The Man: A Farmer's Boy

I Rural Childhood: London Youth

O N December 3, 1766, Robert Bloomfield was born at Honington, a tiny village in Suffolk. George Bloomfield, his father, was penniless, a village tailor who followed his own father's trade.[1] His mother, Elizabeth Manby, daughter of Thomas Manby of Brandon, was the schoolmistress at Honington. They were a proper village couple, virtuous, respectable, and refined: Mr. Narrowback and Mrs. Prim the villagers affectionately named them.[2] Robert was the youngest of their six children.[3]

Before Robert was a full year of age, his father died of smallpox and the family faced even harder times. By continuing as schoolmistress and spinning wool, his mother managed a meager existence for herself and her large family. Her school appears to have been in her home,[4] and she instructed her own children there with her other students.

Honington was a small but attractive village of some two hundred inhabitants, located three miles northwest of Ixworth and seven miles north northwest of Bury St. Edmund's, so Bloomfield's earliest memories were rural ones. Honington was, in the words of a nineteenth-century gazetteer, "pleasantly situated in the vale of a small river,"[5] an agricultural village typical of those which composed the manorial system. In Bloomfield's boyhood it had a large commons, the delight of the Bloomfield children. The village was little changed by 1844 when it boasted two shoemakers, a baker, a blacksmith, a corn miller, a wheelwright, two grocers and drapers, and four farmers.[6]

Robert, like his father, was very small—barely five feet—and never robust. He was, however, a happy child with a quick intellect. If we can trust the memory of his fond oldest brother George for this and the following details, he could read almost before he could walk.

13

Goodie-Two-Shoes and *Jack-The-Giant-Killer* soon gave way to the family copies of the Bible and *Pilgrim's Progress*. Grandfather Manby, who had educated Robert's mother, loaned the family Gray's *Elegy*, Goldsmith's *Deserted Village*, and Watts's *Hymns*. Robert's schooling at his mother's hands, however, left him with a number of inadequacies, and when he was less than seven, his mother with the help of friends managed to send him "to Mr. RODWELL, of Ixworth, to be improved in *Writing*: but he did not go to that School more than two or three months, nor was ever sent to any others."[7]

A very short time later, before Robert turned seven, his mother remarried and as Mrs. Glover added more children to the already crowded household. When Robert was eleven, he was sent to the farm of his mother's new brother-in-law, William Austin of Sapiston. There in the small scattered village with its 1,155 acres of good land, all property and manor of the duke of Grafton, the poet spent his four years as "the farmer's boy." In addition to taking Robert into his house, his uncle paid him the customary one shilling six pence for each week's work, so that his mother had only to find him a few things to wear. "And this," remarks George Bloomfield, "was more than she well knew how to do" (L, vi).

Although Bloomfield was actually too small for heavy farm labor, his life with Mr. Austin was good. For those who might wonder why Bloomfield's Giles, the farmer's boy of the poem, never referred to his relation as "uncle" but always as "Master," George Bloomfield wrote:

The treatment that my Brother *Robert* experienc'd from Mr. *Austin* did not differ in any respect from the treatment that all the Servant Boys experienc'd who lived with him. Mr. *Austin* was father of fourteen Children by my Aunt (he never had any other wife). He left a decent provision for the five Children that surviv'd him: so that it could not be expected he should have any thing to give to poor Relations. And I don't see a possibility of making a difference between GILES and the Boys that were not related to Mr. *Austin:* for he treated all his Servants exactly as he did his Sons. They all work'd hard; all liv'd well. (L, xx–xxi)

Of Mr. Austin, the older brother continued, "The DUKE had not a better Man Tenant to him than the late Mr. *Austin*. I saw numbers of the Husbandmen in tears when he was buried. He was beloved by all who knew him" (L, xxi). The record of Robert's years on this good man's farm is best presented in *The Farmer's Boy* and several other poems. It is sufficient at present to say that Bloomfield did willingly those chores his slight frame would allow and that his quick memory caught accurately the details of the rural life that surrounded him.

Realizing that Robert had no possibility of gaining his livelihood from farm labor, Mr. Austin finally advised his mother that a less taxing trade should be found for him. Robert's oldest brother George, then a shoemaker in London, offered to house him and teach him the trade, while Nathaniel, the next oldest brother and a tailor, offered to clothe him. Thus on June 29, 1781, when Robert was fifteen, he left Mr. Austin's farm and was joined by his mother for the stagecoach journey to London (L, vii).

George was charged by his mother, as he "valued a Mother's Blessing, to watch over him, to set good Examples for him, and never to forget that he had lost his Father" (L, vi–vii). And the eldest brother who became Bloomfield's protector for the next five years described young Robert's entrance into London: "I have him in my mind's eye a little Boy; not bigger than boys generally are at twelve years old. When I met him and his Mother at the Inn, he strutted before us, dress'd just as he came from keeping Sheep, Hogs, &c. . . . his shoes fill'd full of stumps in the heels. He looked about him, slipt up . . . his nails unused to a flat pavement. I remember viewing him as he scamper'd up. . . . how small he was" (L, xxi–xxiii). Later Bloomfield corrected his brother's version of this story:

Now the strict truth of the case is this; that I came (on the 29th of June 1781) in my Sunday-cloaths, such as they were; for I well remember the palpitation of my heart on receiving his proposals to come to town, and how incessantly I thought of the change I was going to experience: Remember well selling my Smock Frock for a Shilling, and slyly washing my best hat in the Horse-pond to give it a gloss fit to appear in the meridian of London. On entering White-Chappel, riding backwards on the coach, a long line of Carriage in the centre of the street attracted my particular notice, and I anxiously look'd for the principle [sic] object in that process of which I concieved [sic] them to be a part, little dreaming that they all stood for hire![8]

George Bloomfield rented lodgings from a Mr. Simm at No. 7,

Pitcher's Court, Bell Alley, Coleman Street, and there he took young Robert:

> It is customary in such houses as are let to poor people in *London*, to have light Garrets fit for Mechanics to work in. In the Garret, where we had two turn-up Beds, and five of us work'd, I received little ROBERT.
> As we were all single Men, Lodgers as a Shilling per week each, our beds were course, and all things being far from clean and snug, like what *Robert* had left at SAPISTON. *Robert* was our man, to fetch all things to hand. At Noon he fetch'd our Dinners from the Cook's Shop: and any one of our fellow workmen that wanted to have any thing fetch'd in, would send him, and assist in his work and teach him, for a recompense for his trouble. (*L*, vii–viii)

A fortunate set of circumstances prevailed which allowed Bloomfield to quicken his understanding of more than Simon Eyre's trade. When the errand boy from the neighboring public house came to collect the men's empty pewter pots and take their orders, he also brought the past day's newspaper. Reading the newspaper aloud, which had been done in turns by the men, soon became the boy's duty, ironically "because his time was of least value." His brother's narrative explains that Robert "frequently met with words that he was unacquainted with: of this he often complained. I one day happen'd at a Book-stall to see a small Dictionary, which had been very ill us'd. I bought it for him for four pence. By the help of this he in a little time could read and comprehend the long and beautiful speeches of Burke, Fox, or North" (*L*, viii). A grand paradox of Bloomfield's life and art, then, may begin here. For the very city he would later abhor as the destroyer of the best of rural life and sensibility, taught him the language of the more conservative writers of the eighteenth century that would become the vehicle for his poetry. And had he been a heartier man, capable of remaining in the countryside to live out his days, what he felt and knew of his rural heritage might never have been written.

Robert's success with the newspapers led in time to more reading aloud. His garret fellows bought him the sixpenny weekly numbers of an *History of England,* the *British Traveler,* and a geography. What he liked best was the more exciting language of the poetry and reviews in the *London Magazine.* His brother suggests (and it is quite possible) that Robert learned there the rudiments of criticism which he would later be capable of using in his offhand way. Even more important, however, was his keen interest in the Poet's Corner.

If the routine of learning his trade and waiting on his companions in a dingy garret weighed heavily on a boy enchanted by England's rural beauty, there were Sundays on which he could explore the city or walk out to the country, ". . . beyond the sweep/Of London's congregated cloud."[9] George Bloomfield records a new excitement that began one Sunday after Robert's temporary escape from the fuliginous streets:

> [W]e by accident went into a dissenting *Meeting-house,* in the *Old Jewry,* where a Gentleman was lecturing. This man fill'd *Robert* with astonishment. The House was amazingly crowded with the most genteel people: and though we were forc'd to stand in the aisle, and were much press'd, yet *Robert* always quicken'd his steps to get into Town on a Sunday evening soon enough to attend this Lecture. (*L,* viii–ix)

The Reverend Mr. Fawcet, a poet, and a lecturer of considerable popularity, had what was to George's ear language "just such as the *Rambler* is written in," and, finding his delivery and presence that of an actor in a tragedy, George pronounced "his Discourse rational, and free from the Cant of Methodism." "Of him," George states, "*Robert* learn'd to accent what he call'd *hard* words; and otherwise improv'd himself; and gain'd the most enlarg'd notions of *Providence*" (*L,* ix). The willingness of a rural lad to educate and "improve" himself in such circumstances may not be remarkable, but what is surprising and ultimately more important is that Bloomfield would not be trapped by a false humility into mindlessly mimicking the language and thought he encountered. His other experiences with public speakers during his years with George were limited to a few visits to a Debating Society at Coachmaker's Hall and an occasional trip to Covent Garden.

By the mid-1780s, Bloomfield's interest in the "Poet's Corner" became a more personal one, and he attempted to place his first poetic endeavors in the *London Magazine.* His early productions were apparently composed in his mind while he cobbled. "A Village Girl," a ditty of small merit which appeared in Say's *Gazetteer* on May 24, 1786, is in many ways representative of his first attempts. With "The Sailor's Return" and several other brief pieces, "The Village Girl" serves mainly as a record that the shoemaker had begun to give his all to poetry some time before he composed *The Farmer's Boy*.[10]

II An Apprenticeship: Continuing Education

Around 1783, another fortunate circumstance served the haphazard advance of Robert's education. His facility with language had improved so much that he was offering instruction to his brother and the others in the garret, when a new man came to their lodgings who prompted the Bloomfield brothers to find new quarters. The new lodger was afflicted with fits, which from George Bloomfield's account could be judged epileptic seizures. The contortions and screams which marked the attacks greatly excited Robert's sympathy for the man. Unable to help or calm himself, however, Bloomfield found living near the man impossible. A move to Blue Hart Court, Bell Alley, provided the young poet with an essential prerequisite to the creation of *The Farmer's Boy*:

> In our new Garret we found a singular character, *James Kay*, a native of *Dundee*. He was a middle-aged man, of a good understanding, and yet a furious *Calvinist*. He had many Books,—and some which he did not value; such as the *Seasons, Paradise Lost*, and some *Novels*. These BOOKS he lent to ROBERT: who spent all his leisure hours reading the *Seasons*, which he was now capable of reading. I never heard him give so much praise to any Book as to that. (*L*, xii–xiii)

Bloomfield, without the benefit of a formal education and without personal wealth which might have given him the leisure necessary for extensive self-education, was writing verse, however crude, and appreciating Milton and Thomson in his eighteenth year. He was not seduced by any false notion of his capabilities, and he thought of himself, still, as a shoemaker. There were years of learning, experience, and seasoning to come before Bloomfield would essay anything so ambitious as *The Farmer's Boy*.

In 1784, a labor dispute involving Robert was resolved only after he had fled the city for a time. The journeymen shoemakers, in an attempt to protect their position in the trade, objected to the practice of employing men who had learned without an apprenticeship. The Bloomfields' employer in Cheapside, a Mr. Chamberlayne, actively opposed the journeymen, going so far as to buy off his employees who affiliated themselves with the journeymen's clubs. "This so exasperated the men," wrote George Bloomfield, "that their acting Committee soon look'd for *unlawful men* (as they called them) among *Chamberlayne's* workmen" (*L,* xiii).

Robert had served no apprenticeship. When he was discovered, the Committee of the Lawful Crafts threatened both Chamberlayne, for employing him, and George Bloomfield, for teaching him, with prosecution. While Chamberlayne was urging George to bring the matter to trial and offering to support the case, George became involved in a personal conflict with a member of the journeymen's committee.

Disturbed by the quarrels around him and fearing for his brother's personal safety, Robert withdrew to the country where he was taken in by Mr. Austin. In all probability, he would have returned to his home in Honington, but his mother, her family, and school had been driven from the house by fire in 1783 and his stepfather had died only months earlier.[11] If we trust George Bloomfield's account of the period, Robert's two-month stay in the country excited and reaffirmed his affection for the rural life. Thomson's writings were a recent excitement, and they may have structured his vision of his native country. It was a time of romance, too. Bloomfield fell in love with Nancy Bantock of Broadmere. However, though the romance was renewed when he visited Honington again two years later, it eventually ended and she married a local man.[12]

Although the trade dispute remained unsettled, Robert's affairs were improved considerably. He returned to London and, through a bit of subterfuge, the legal form of the apprenticeship was met.[13] Bloomfield had his brother's guidance and company for two more years as he perfected his shoemaking. In 1786 when Robert was twenty and skilled at his craft, George left him living alone in London and making his own way.

One of the earliest of Bloomfield's remaining letters was written to Mr. Austin during this period. In it he speaks of his invitation to Austin's two sons for a brief stay with him in London. Rayner Unwin, remarking that the letter shows little precocity or confidence, asserts that Robert's seven years in London had been "sheltered and unadventurous."[14] The tone of the letter in which Bloomfield complains of the cramped alley in which he lives, the dangers of traveling the streets at night and of frequenting "low lived places," and the difficulty of finding lodgings, especially for women, seems to support Mr. Unwin's contention.[15] Yet it may be that Unwin has accepted the rather sad, bland, stereotyped vision of

Bloomfield fostered by Victorian preface writers. A more devious mind could find the letter to be exactly what a young man in the city would write to his uncle on the impending visit of his cousins—a letter that would allay all the gentlemen's fears, even those about the youths' behavior. The dangers of the streets at night could be avoided, Bloomfield wrote, by staying off them. Low lived places the boys would shun, ". . . and so long as we do so, there is no danger to be feared." And there was some discussion of a female cousin joining the youths in the city—a possibility which Bloomfield eliminated by telling his uncle of the impossibility of finding lodgings for a young lady.

III   A Marriage and a Poem

It is known that after George left London, Robert found a lively interest in music and played the violin. He sold one of his hand-crafted aeolian harps to the Scottish poet James Montgomery. His interest in romance must have quickened too, for within four years he wrote to his brother that he "had sold his Fiddle and got a Wife" (L, xvi). Indeed, on December 12, 1790, Bloomfield married Mary-Anne Church, the daughter of a shipbuilder in the government yard at Woolwich. The young couple first lived in furnished lodgings while struggling to assemble some possessions of their own. Before the Bloomfields had found the financial stability necessary for furnishing new quarters, their first child, Hannah, was born on October 25, 1791.[16]

The following year, Bloomfield hired a second-story room at 14 Bell Alley, Coleman Street, where the growing family was to live for seven years. Their landlords, the Hortons, allowed Robert to work in a garret two stories above the room, but with rent of seven pounds per year, the Bloomfields often found themselves in arrears (MS 28,268, 19–20).

In May, 1796, Robert, now father of two daughters, began to compose his best poem, The Farmer's Boy. Aware as he was of the public association of him with Burns, he later dated the beginning of composition as two months before Burns died. Bloomfield himself describes the effort:

When I began it, I thought to myself that I could compleat it in a twelvemonth, allowing myself three months for each quarter; but I soon found that I could not, and indeed I made it longer than I first intended.

Nine tenths of it was put together as I sat at work, where there are usually six of us; no one in the house has any knowledge of what I have employed my thoughts about when I did not talk.

I chose to do it in rhime for this reason; because I found always that when I put two or three lines together in blank verse, or something that sounded like it, it was a great chance if it stood right when it came to be wrote down, for blank verse has ten-syllables in a line, and this particular I could not adjust, nor bear in memory as I could rhimes. Winter, and half of Autumn were done long before I could find leisure to write them. (MS 28,266, 85r–85v).

He finished the poem in April, 1798.

It was Bloomfield's first intention that the poem be nothing more than a present for his mother. It was a memento of his childhood, including much that would be familiar to her. But, as he wrote to his brother,

When I had nearly done it, it came strongly into my mind that very silly things are sometimes printed, but by what means I know not. To try to get at this knowledge I resolved to make some efforts of that sort; and, what encouraged me to go through with it was, that if I got laugh'd at, no one that I cared for could know it, unless I myself told them. I sometimes thought of venturing it into the house of some person above a Bookseller, but I never could find impudence enough to do it. (MS 28,266, 86)

Bloomfield, however, did screw up his courage and carry the manuscript to a "Magazine-man" his brother had apparently mentioned to him. In a letter that accompanied the manuscript, Bloomfield described himself and his reasons for writing the poem, and asked "whether the little pieces, particularly Autumn, and Winter, contain anything like poetical merit. That is to say, to what excellence in others it makes the nearest approach" (MS 28,266, 86). Realizing that his "Magazine-man" might be less than interested in an unsolicited manuscript from a journeyman shoemaker, he proposed to come for it in a fortnight. The gentleman, Mr. W. Bent, publisher of the *Universal Magazine* which George had read for years, kept the poem for better than a week, then had it and a note carried back by "a sober-looking book-faced man." The note said simply, "*The Farmer's Boy* may afford pleasure to the person for whom it is intended; but it cannot be expected that any stranger should give his opinion of such a literary performance to the author" (MS 28,266, 87r).

Still hopeful, Bloomfield wrote a shorter letter to send with the manuscript to Mr. William Lane, "the wholesale novel manufacturer."[17] Realizing the financial risk to a publisher in bringing out fifteen hundred lines of verse by an unknown laborer, Bloomfield asked "whether there is any probability of its repaying you, Sir, or myself the expense of publication" (MS 28, 266, 87v). The shoemaker may have thought his chances of publication better if the publisher had no expense, for he went on to indicate his willingness to stand the cost and confessed his ignorance of what that might be. Lane's brief but courteous reply, however, was that ". . . as poetry is quite out of his line, he begs to decline it" (MS 28, 266, 88).

Robert next sent the poem to Mr. Charles Dilly "in the Poultry" with a copy of the same letter he had sent to Mr. Lane. Again, he had no success but did get Dilly's recommendation that he attempt to publish the poem in a magazine. Bloomfield did not follow that advice, first, because he did not wish to buy his own verses as they appeared in the numbers of the magazine, and second, because it might have taken six months to see it all in print. Unable to find out either the cost of printing the poem or what its merits might be, Bloomfield left the book to be enjoyed by his brother and friends and quit his direct efforts to shepherd it into print (MS 28, 266, 90). It was George Bloomfield, then, who found *The Farmer's Boy* its first and most valuable patron.

IV   A *Patron for* The Farmer's Boy

Six and one half miles from Bury St. Edmund's, where the eldest Bloomfield brother then followed his trade, stands Troston Hall, the manor to the village of Troston and for a time the seat of the Capel and Lofft families. Edward Capel, writer, Shakesperian commentator, and deputy inspector of plays, was born there in 1713. It was to his nephew, Capel Lofft, who had become lord of the manor, that George Bloomfield carried the manuscript of the poem. Lofft was a barrister who enjoyed a fair reputation as a writer on legal and political matters. He was also something of a man of letters who had earned a local fame as a patron of the arts that Byron would lampoon in *English Bards and Scotch Reviewers*.

Lofft's response was both cordial and encouraging. Soon after receiving the manuscript in November, 1798, he sent it to his friend Thomas Hill, who concurred with Lofft on the poem's merits. Hill put the manuscript in the hands of the publishers Vernor and Hood who agreed to publish it. In befriending the author and offering him at last some critical estimate of the poem, Lofft was an almost ideal patron. In an age which still had, at least from custom, some literary prejudice against the writings of the poor and the self-educated, Lofft indicated that he found both merit and social significance in *The Farmer's Boy:*

The example, as well as the poem, may teach the rich, and the highly born or educated, not unnaturally to urge harsh and overbearing lines of distinctions but to be more attentive to the gifts bestowed by the common Father on mankind, than to an overweening conceit of their own priviledges [*sic*] and advantages.

Their priviledges [*sic*] and advantages would amply gain in good will and security what they might thus sacrifice from the cold and degrading claims of unfeeling ostentation. (MS 28, 266, 92)

After correcting the manuscript for grammar and orthography, Lofft wrote, "The corrections, in point of grammar, reduce themselves almost wholly to a circumstance of provincial usage, which even well-educated persons in SUFFOLK and NORFOLK do not wholly avoid; and which may be said, as to general custom, to have become in these counties almost an establish'd Dialect:—that of adopting the plural for the singular termination of verbs, so as to exclude the *s*" (*L*, xix). It was Lofft, too, who inspected the proofs and guided the poem through its lengthy stay at the printer.

For Bloomfield, the first promise of success (and success to him remained having a printed copy of his poem for his mother) stirred terror as well as joy. Beset by illnesses, the expenses of a growing family, and the effort of simply getting on, he looked back somewhat wistfully to the years of the poem's composition. A suppressed section of a letter to his brother in 1799 shows a bit of the man soon hidden away by his editors and biographers:

My wife and I agree that during the two years that I was breeding with Giles [the "farmer's boy" of the poem] we got on smoother than before, our girls were boath [*sic*] out of hand, our rest was sound, etc., but it unfortunately happened that by the time I was brought to bed with my Boy, my wife was breeding another; we some times see a ball of wax with so small a portion of the boyant [*sic*] quality that it knows not whither to sink or swim; if you put your finger on it when at the surfice [*sic*], it will dive deep and be a long time in rising again; so it was with my Boy Charles, he dived me into some debts this time twelvemonth, from which I am not yet free, but I have great hopes I shall be free by the end of November. It is true we

are no shining part of the community.—They go to market with the fruit of
other people's labour, and then with a double chalk score it up to their own
industry and hard striving. (MS 28,266, 19r–19v)

In the same letter, he spoke whimsically of the new lodgings he
had found for his family:

We now hired on the spot, a dining room, bedroom, kitchen, washhouse,
nursery, workshop, etc.; that is to say a large two pair stairs room, with two
north windows and one south, at No. 1 Mulberry Court, our north prospect
is terminated by a high range of chimney-pots in Coleman Street buildings,
but here is a thorough air (cockney air) & excellent light. All our endeavours
are to get clear, and to live happy, and to hope humbly, and thereby blunt
the edge of disappointment. (MS 28,268, 20r)

This last he offered for George's wife who, like others, feared that
the prospect of a literary reputation might weaken Robert's efforts at
shoemaking and fill him with foolish expectations. Not unaware of
such dangers, Bloomfield at first resolved to count any income from
his poem as an incidental blessing.

During the fifteen months that elapsed while the poem was being
printed, Bloomfield knew little of its progress. He had good faith in
the judgment of Capel Lofft and Mr. Hood, the more active of the
publishing partners, and seldom bothered to enquire about their
work. Still, his "Boy" was not out of mind. "I remember feeling
much anxiety," he wrote, perhaps in fear of losing his creation, "and
(having the poem then perfect in my memory) after a hard day's
work, with my back to the fire, and in the stillness of the night I had
often repeated aloud the whole, or greater part of the poem, untile
[sic] my wife was fast asleep, before I could find resolution to put out
the candle" (MS 28,266, 92v). His trepidations, however great,
would actually increase after the poem appeared in the shops in
March, 1800.

That Bloomfield knew more of his poem's progress by the time of
its publication is doubtful, for he wrote that it was his brother
Nathaniel who reported seeing in a shop window "a book call'd
'The Farmer's Boy' with a Motto" (MS 28,266, 93). Although the
appearance of the "Motto" ("A Shepherd's Boy—he seeks no better
name," the first line of Pope's "Summer, The Second Pastoral, or
Alexis") was surprising to Bloomfield, it was not so awesome as his
next experience as a published poet. The duke of Grafton, lord of
the manor to both Honington and Sapiston, was in Picadilly, and he

summoned Robert for an audience. Although nervous and confused, the poet was inevitably pleased: "I met with condescention [*sic*] in its noblest features, and even with congratulations. And amidst the conversation was very naturally ask'd 'how I liked the execution of the work?' 'was it not beautifully printed?' I replied that I had not yet seen it. The Duke himself then brought from the Library one of the large paper copies, and spread it on the table. Giles never was so hard put in his life to keep his face in order as at that moment" (MS 28,266, 93r–93v). Happily, Bloomfield's reaction to such events was humor and whimsy, not the fawning that circumstance might have forced on him.

Similarly, what might have become conceit in a less balanced man was replaced in Bloomfield by humility and a troublesome but unaffected shyness. The paradox of humility and shyness mixing with excitement about his work and its potential success makes instructive reading of his letters. When the early success of *The Farmer's Boy* brought invitations for interviews, teas, and dinner, Bloomfield's complaints about embarrassment, lost time and income, and shrinking privacy were just as numerous as his remarks of pleasure. Vocal as he was about his frustration with the demands of his public, he kept by his side "a Book of memorandums" recording his visits and shared any literary man's concern with exactly what posterity should know of his life and letters (MS 28,266, 93v).

The Farmer's Boy, then, was a success. On March 5, 1800, Bloomfield was able to send a copy to his mother. Contrary to his better judgment, he indulged himself with hope of improving the situation of his family with the earnings of his book. The first income was a present of five guineas from the duke of Grafton (MS 28,266, 94v). Bloomfield, who was delighted with that sum, could write to his brother in October, 1800, that the first three editions of the poem were handled at a cost of 481 pounds and would bring a profit of 613 pounds when sold. In addition to half of any profit, the publisher had also promised to give Bloomfield a part of his own profits—fifty pounds and fifty more from the next three editions. This was altogether 100 pounds more than the poet had expected.

By the fall of 1800, Mrs. Bloomfield was pregnant once more, and the poet began casting about for some employment that would improve his income. He discussed with Lofft and the duke of Grafton his plans to become a master shoemaker, decided against a position in Bury (apparently as keeper of an inn), and thought better of opening a shop in London (MS 28,268, 41r–42r). The letters between Robert and George for the next years continued full of shoemaking talk as Robert began to sell his own wares and keep his own accounts. By the early months of 1801, Robert had employed a man half-time to assist him in the trade. It was his other life, however, that became the real center of his existence.

Soon Bloomfield was posing for portraits, hearing of a Latin translation of the first quarter of his poem, and discovering more and more the irksome nature of life as a public man.[18] It was natural that Mr. Lofft, Mr. Austin, and even the duke of Grafton should be central figures in his life, and the poet enjoyed for the best part his visits and correspondence with them. It was also natural, however, that others from the nobility, the gentry, the literary world, and the curious public in general should make demands on his time and ultimately on his resources. He spent, for example, a fruitless day with Sir Charles Bunbury waiting to see the prince of Wales, visited for a week with Dr. Nathan Drake of Hadleigh—who in his *Literary Hours* was an early champion of Bloomfield's poetry—and found himself at home to a chequered parade of minor literary figures who brought him copies of their works. But his poetry thus far failed to support him, and his time for shoemaking was devoured by his literary life. Of his inability to serve two masters, he wrote to his brother, "I think I could manage *one* very well . . . I have hither to [*sic*] known my ——— from my head, which is sometimes (now) as much as I can say" (MS 28,268, 52).

By November, 1801, his situation was worse. Still without any permanent or regular income, he wrote that "if the edge of public curiosity should wear off I may have uninterrupted Leisure; though by my daily increasing popularity I ought not to reason so. I try to select my acquaintance, and there is need of it" (MS 28,268, 76r). Bloomfield's complaint continued even in the years of relative prosperity.

Throughout the early years of Bloomfield's career as a poet, his prospects for a permanent income were consistently mercuric as were his reactions to them. He depended for a time on what income he could get from shoemaking and selling copies of his songs. The growth of his family and the necessity of moving to a house on City Road in the Shepherdess Walk helped absorb the first income from his book. His few luxuries included books, pictures, some good mahogany furniture, and a Hawkins patent writing machine (an early typewriter).[19] In August, 1801, he had enough money at hand to lend his brother George fifty pounds, but consequently by

September he was forced to apply to his publisher for an advance. He felt, at that point, that if the duke of Grafton or some kind patron would employ him regularly at eighty pounds per year, he could soon save five hundred pounds (MS 28,268, 55–57).

V   A *Second Success:* Rural Tales, Ballads, and Songs

Despite his vexations, Bloomfield had composed the poetry for his second volume, *Rural Tales, Ballads, and Songs,* by the fall of 1801. These early years of his career were, in fact, the most productive, and from 1796 to 1811 he wrote most of what would finally compose his canon. In 1798 and 1799 he wrote most of the pieces in *Rural Tales* in odd seasonal bouts, composing almost all the poems from the spring to the fall of the year.[20]

What security the publication of a new book might have promised him, however, was shaken for a time by a bitter quarrel between Lofft, Bloomfield, and Thomas Hood. Wedged between patron and publisher in the affair, the poet took to his bed suffering a rheumatic attack in his shoulder and the recurrence of an old stomach complaint. "If they would let me alone," he snapped, "I might live as long as any of them; but they place me awkardly in their quarrels: Genious [sic] is not wanted to work my extrication, but Jockyship, constitutional vigor, and impudence" (MS 28,268, 75r).

Conflict between Lofft and Hood was not new. This time it was prompted by Bloomfield's wish to remove Lofft's inappropriate political notes from the end of future editions of *The Farmer's Boy* and to withhold the patron's "notes of approbation" which were to precede each poem in *Rural Tales.* Lofft thought this to be the work of Hood, who he was sure wished his name and influence completely removed from Bloomfield's works. Despite the quarrel, the new issue of *The Farmer's Boy* was at hand and *Rural Tales* was soon to come; Bloomfield's prospects seemed excellent. He wrote to his brother, "The fifth and sixth editions of 'Giles' comprise together 10,000 copies, and the new work 7,000, so that I have at any rate to share the profits of 17,000 books, for which (at full price) the public, if they are good-natured enough to buy them, will pay no less than £36,025" (C, 17). The surprising and yet typical reaction of the poet to his success follows: "I have felt sad, and uncommon trouble of mind; and I doubt it is over yet."

Rural Tales was still at press in November, 1801, when the sixth edition of *The Farmer's Boy* was arranged. In deference to Lofft's distressed feelings, Bloomfield quietly overrode the wishes of the publishers and brought the edition to the public with Lofft's political notes intact. Bloomfield insisted that the disputed notes in *Rural Tales* remain in the small octavo editions, but allowed the publisher to remove them from the quarto and large octavo copies (MS 28,268, 451). The two formats of *Rural Tales, Ballads, and Songs* appeared in a first edition in January, 1802.[21]

Aware now of his relationship with the public and his role as a writer, he carefully directed the printing of his poetry and fretted with the delays. "No dying lover in a romance," he wrote, "ever longed for the bridal-day more sincerely or fervently than I do for the birth of my volume" (*C*, 18). The man who now quoted Burns and read with excitement whatever new books appeared in London was confident enough of his abilities and his fortune as a poet to be angry when George reported that gossips were predicting his ruin: "If you hear any more stories, tell them that three years will produce me £1,000, besides £150 in considerations. Tell them that I have signed and exchanged agreements for my children's sake; that for fourteen years I have to expect a good annuity: and tell 'em that if I live fourteen years the whole is my own again. And lastly tell 'em, dam' 'em—for I don't care nothing about 'em, &c., &c., &c." (*C*, 19). When his new poems at last were ready, Robert wrote proudly telling his brother to "stroke your beard, and lift your leg, and rejoice" (*C*, 20).

For a time, Bloomfield seemed to enjoy his success. An annuity of fifteen pounds a year from the duke of Grafton, the income from his two books, and what he could contrive from shoemaking and a continuing enterprise, constructing and selling aeolian harps, gave him some peace. W. W. Wickett describes Bloomfield's life at this point:

On many occasions the Duke of Grafton welcomed him at his Piccadilly house, where he saw again, amongst other celebrities, the Prince Regent and Beau Brummel and, no doubt the actress Mrs. Siddons as well as the poetess, Mrs. Anna Laetitia Barbauld, and Mrs. Elizabeth Inchbald, the actress-daughter of a Stanningfield, Suffolk, farmer. The Prince entertained him several times at Carlton House, where he met Mrs. Fitzherbert, the Prince's companion until 1803. Bloomfield would sometimes give a demonstration of his prodigious memory to those present.[22]

By this account, Bloomfield, who now had *The Seasons, The Castle of Indolence,* and most of Burns by heart, would repeat great passages of poetry from books he had just seen and was surprised that his memory should draw the attention of others.

He continued a great correspondence, sometimes resorting to a "Diary" which he could mail to his family and to friends (MS 28,268, 83). He read, followed his reviews, and visited, at one point wistfully declining an invitation by the earl of Buchan to visit Scotland for the double reason that "Burns is dead, or I might have seen him [and]—I am married" (*C*, 23).

A position which might have provided the security and income the poet desired was finally offered to him late in 1802. The duke of Grafton appointed Bloomfield to the position of undersealer in the King's Bench Court. But the man who loved quiet and the country and who had little constitutional vigor was ill suited to the cluttered, crowded frenzy of the Seal Office. By the end of February, 1803, Robert was writing to his brother of his vexations (*C*, 30). In the *Morning Chronicle* he read that "Bloomfield, the poet, has been recently appointed to a *handsome* [italics Bloomfield's] situation in the Seal Office in the Temple: thus he has not courted the Muses unsuccessfully." From George he learned of a similar story in the Bury paper (*C*, 30). The *Herald* first had the same news, but soon announced that he had resigned when he had not. " 'Tis useless to be angry," he fumed to the widowed George, "but if the asses that meddle with another man's business before they know it were buried three times as deep as your poor wife, I would not wear black for them" (*C*, 30).

On May 27, 1803, he wrote that four more months like the past four at the Seal Office would drive him mad,[23] and he determined to seal his last writ at seven the following day. With some resignation he wrote, "I value the world's applause; [*sic*] more than it's [*sic*] pity, and therefore says I to the Lawyers 'Goodbye' " (MS 28,268, 126).

It was unfortunate, as George Bloomfield reminisced in 1827, that the poet lacked the proper health and emotional nature for the post. Mr. Allen, his superior, lived only a short time, and it is quite probable that the duke of Grafton would have made Bloomfield master sealer.[24]

What income Bloomfield did have, it was his nature to share. He made efforts at this point to improve the lot of his old mother. His earliest surviving letters to her carried what money he could spare, and in May, 1802, he wrote to George about the possibility of having a new thatched roof over their "old friend in Honington" (MS

28,268, 95). The following month he sent the necessary money to his brother who would oversee the roofing. In July Bloomfield persuaded her to come to London for what would be her last visit.

Soon after her return to Honington, her health began to wane. Around December 17 she was taken seriously ill. Robert quit a holiday in the country and was at her side on the twentieth. His memories of the woman for whom *The Farmer's Boy* was written, catch some of the same tone used in his fond descriptions of the old, rural poor:

> During the period of evident decline in her strength and facilities, she conceived, in place of that patient resignation which she has before felt, an ungovernable dread of ultimate want, and observed to a relative with peculiar emphasis, that "to meet WINTER, OLD AGE, and POVERTY, was like meeting three great giants."
>
> To the last hour of her life she was an excellent spinner; and latterly, the peculiar kind of wool which she spun was brought exclusively for her, as being the only one in the village who exercised their industry on so fine a sort. During the tearful paroxysms of her last depression she spun with utmost violence, and with vehemence exclaimed—"*I must spin!*" A paralytic affection struck her whole right side while at work, and obliged her to quit her spindle when only half filled, and she died within a fortnight afterwards.[25]

A generosity that many considered foolish prompted Bloomfield to provide an estate for her heirs, purchase the title of her cottage for his stepfather, and spend altogether more than a year's income from the duke of Grafton on her care and funeral.

The pain of his mother's death was not Bloomfield's only misfortune of the year. His son Charles, who was born with *The Farmer's Boy*, had not been a healthy child. In February, 1803, the boy developed a "white swelling" on his knee that recurred with such intensity as to make him lame (MS 28,268, 53ff.). Soon the affliction was complicated by convulsions which left the child senseless. Shortly after the death of his mother as Bloomfield saw his son's condition become more grave, and he arranged for his wife to take the boy to the seaside where a cure might be effected. In July, the poet joined his wife and son at Worthing where he penned delightful letters to his daughter Hannah and his father-in-law, who had also become a part of the already large household (MS 28,268, 187–90). The cure was not totally effective, and Charles was still lame in 1806 when Bloomfield dedicated his *Wild Flowers* to him.

Bloomfield's reactions to these events is in a way curious. There is no doubt of his affection and concern for family: he gave willingly of his affection, his time, and his income. But he managed domestic tragedy with greater dignity and acceptance than he did his literary disappointments. I suspect that in his mind his family was associated with the natural, the rural, the known, while his literary career (as opposed to his poetry) was inevitably connected to the city. From one he drew his strength; the other sapped his vitality. That pattern becomes more clear later as we see him curse the city while continuing his lifelong habit of retreat to the countryside.

Bloomfield's character in 1804 was, despite his financial difficulties, that of an independent, confident man. That he was no slave to patronage, money, or influence is demonstrated by a remarkable occurrence in the spring of that year. A young man who signed himself only as "B. C." wrote asking Bloomfield to ghostwrite an elegy on the recent death of a successful and wealthy captain in the Royal Navy. The youth's letter, which described the character of the captain in some detail, explained that he had not himself the necessary skill in poetry but was being urged by his friends to produce an elegy. For inducement, he enclosed half of a ten pound note with the promise of the other half whem Bloomfield delivered the elegy. "I know you to be a man of honour," wrote B. C., "and the advantages which I might soon derive will certainly enable me to make you a much more liberal compensation . . ." (*C*, 34–35). Despite B. C.'s assurance that the bribe was simply a present for the enjoyment Bloomfield's poetry had afforded him, the poet was insulted and he replied to the young man immediately.

"It is a matter of utmost astonishment to me," Bloomfield began, "that any man could for a moment trust his reputation in the keeping of a stranger in the manner you propose to do with me. Granting that you may be right when you call me *a man of honour*, you probably mean that I would keep the secret if I bound myself to it. But to what man of honour would a sensible stranger offer the wages of prostitution?" (*C*, 35). Bloomfield's tone became sharper as he came onto his subject properly:

Whatever may be your views and expectations as to the property of the worthy officer you wish to praise in verse, I beg of you to consider that the celebration of candour, truth, and sincerity in him would be an everlasting reproach on yourself who would appear to the world to have paid a debt of justice to the dead, while your conscience would only have this poor consolation, that by the bait of wealth you have made another man as great a rogue and fool as yourself. (*C*, 35)

Bloomfield returned the ten pound note wishing the fellow success in all honest endeavors. Later, "B. C." tried to right the situation through the offices of Joseph Bancroft, who wrote apologetically to Bloomfield to ask for the return of all the letters involved, sending yet another bank note as a present. Bloomfield in an improved humor complied, but returned the money. The father of five children, he thought, could well have some generous feelings for the impertinences of youth.

VI *Bloomfield in the Literary World*

Despite the initial hardships during the middle period of his career, and despite his constitutional aversion to public life, the poet's education in the ways of London's literary society and of the world at large continued. In addition to Capel Lofft, the duke of Grafton, and Dr. Nathan Drake, he was acquainted to varying degrees with Charles Lamb, Dr. Edward Jenner, George Dyer (who introduced him to Lamb and others), Robert Southey, Samuel Rogers, George Crabbe, William Holloway, James Montgomery, Bernard Barton, and later John Clare. His library included presentation copies of works from a host of minor literary figures. His patrons, led by the duke of Grafton, contributed numerous volumes they thought the poet should read. In addition to contemporary books of sermons, grammar, biography, arithmetic, natural history, travel and topography, and hymns, Bloomfield's shelves soon contained Pope, Johnson, Dryden, Butler, Gay, Spenser, Goldsmith, Shenstone, Gray, Burns, Cowper, Richard Cumberland, Shakespeare, Milton, Browne, Temple, Homer, Virgil, and Thomson, as well as many of his contemporaries including Southey, Scott, Wordsworth, Coleridge, Kirke White, Mrs. Opie, Mrs. Barbauld, Crabbe, and Gilpin.[26]

Shortly after the publication of *The Farmer's Boy*, Robert Southey, who was abroad at the actual time of its publication, returned and began writing reviews in *The Critical Review*, one of which was of *The Farmer's Boy*. Later in a letter to Coleridge, Southey mentions having seen Bloomfield in London: "An interesting man he is—even more than you would expect."[27] The poem, which he once thought "most miraculously over-rated," he reviewed kindly. His express aim in the review was to further Bloomfield's career, although he wondered exactly how Bloomfield might be brought to any critical touchstone. Years later, after Bloomfield's affairs had collapsed, Southey actively sought a solution to the poet's financial desperation, proposing several plans by which Bloomfield might offset his losses and attempting to raise funds from the booksellers. Even after Bloomfield's death, Southey championed his name and sought a place for him in literary history. Only advanced years prevented the poet laureate from publishing his proposed study of "one whose talents were of no common standard."[28]

If Bloomfield had champions in Southey and Lofft, he was no less a champion himself to another of his notable acquaintances. Having lost his father and several other family members to smallpox, Bloomfield was particularly receptive to the then controversial ideas of Dr. Edward Jenner. The poet began as early as the winter of 1800 to have his children vaccinated. Despite the four attempts necessary for a successful innoculation of his daughter Mary, his confidence in Jenner's vaccine continued, and in October, 1801, he had his youngest child vaccinated (MS 28,268, 69). In January, 1802, he wrote to Dr. Nathan Drake, "What think you of the Vaccine? Is it not a glorious cause?" (*C*, 20). It is possible that he had begun his poem on the subject, "Good Tidings; or, News from the Farm."

Although it is impossible at this point to determine just how the poet came to know Dr. Jenner, they had met by the summer of 1802. In July of that year Bloomfield wrote to his brother:

I have seen Dr. Jenner, and his kindness almost induced me to show him the little progress I have made in pursuit of his subject; but I suddenly determined to the contrary, and doubted the propriety of so doing. This moment a letter from Dr. Jenner invites me to tea this evening. What shall I do—leave 150 lines of an unfinished subject in his hands? I am bound to consult Mr. Lofft and the Duke, and to submit my pieces to their judgement, and never will do otherwise; and yet it is hard to say *no* in such cases as this. I wish he would suspend his curiosity six months, and I would take my chance. He is a very amiable man, and perhaps rates my abilities too high. He is an enthusiast in his pursuit, and well he may, when it is taken up by every country in Europe, and by the poor Cherokees of America. The blessing is surely immensely great! and has features of an uncommon kind. Did you ever give it your serious consideration? or am I upon a wrong scent? Do I

———— fault'ring quit the pack,
Snuff the foul scent, and hasten yelping back?

I pray God send it the confirmation of experience! and the gratitude not by
the humble efforts of your affectionate brother. (C, 28–29)

In November of the same year, Bloomfield's brother Nat lost a
third child to smallpox. When the smallpox eruptions appeared on
the baby of the same family, Bloomfield took his nephew Tom, who
had thus far escaped the disease, into his own home and resolved to
have the boy vaccinated. "I am inexpressably [sic] hurt and confounded at this stroke," he wrote, "and it shall operate as a powerful
stimulous [sic] on my Mind in pursuit of that great and Momentus
[sic] Subject" (MS 28,268, 113).

Jenner was in London again in February, 1803, and exchanged
letters with Bloomfield (MS 28,268, 118). The following month at a
celebration in honor of Jenner's birthday, Bloomfield sang a song he
had composed for the occasion.[29] "Good Tidings" was evidently in
its finished state in July, for Dr. Nathan Drake had seen it and had
written a preface for it, and Bloomfield and Lofft were in the happy
process of discarding the first title, "Vaccine Rose." Lofft suggested
"Vaccine Inoculation," but Bloomfield may have favored "On Vacci-
nation," for it was by that title that Jenner enquired after the poem's
progress in August (C, 33).

When the poem was published in 1804, Bloomfield was invited to
recite from it at the anniversary meeting of the Royal Jennerian
Society. Thus, for the second year the poet celebrated the doctor's
birthday (May 17) with verse. While on an excursion along the Wye
in the summer of 1807, Bloomfield called on Jenner at Cheltenham,
and the good doctor sent along a tea caddy as a present for Mrs.
Bloomfield (C, 147). Nothing more of their relationship can be
gleaned from the poet's letters. Among the poet's effects sold at
auction after his death, however, was a silver inkstand "presented to
Mr. R. Bloomfield by the celebrated Dr. Jenner."[30] What is
perhaps most important here, is that Bloomfield, humble as his
origins were and "uneducated" as he was, recognized the importance to humanity of Jenner's work. Although he was attracted to
the "rural" nature of the treatment, his sophistication was such that
he researched the work of Jenner's co-worker, William Woodville,
arming himself for more than a sentimental and emotional argu-

ment. Creating the poem and vaccinating his family are both demonstrations of a man acting upon his beliefs.

The initial effect of Bloomfield's support for Jenner's cause is difficult to weigh. The separate edition of "Good Tidings" was evidently not too successful in the bookshops, and Bloomfield complained that the booksellers did not advertise it because they did not own it. The poet could not or would not advertise it himself (MS 28,268, 149). When the poem was "improved" and included in the 1806 edition of *Wild Flowers; or, Pastoral and Local Poetry*, however, it reached a most respectable audience.

VII *Composing* Wild Flowers *and Touring The Wye*

In examining Bloomfield's career following the completion of "Good Tidings," it becomes even apparent that he was most productive during his late thirties and early forties. When he had finished the pieces for *Rural Tales* and was awaiting its completion by the printers, he had amused himself with the writing of a children's tale, *The History of Little Davy's New Hat*. The tale was in a form finished enough to be sent to his brother and shown to Capel Lofft early in 1802 (*C*, 72), but the poet was working on it again in 1803 (MS 28,268, 136). Other interests, however, claimed his attention, and it was not until 1815 that the work was published.

While he revised his celebration of Dr. Jenner's vaccine, Bloomfield was also writing the other pieces that would appear in *Wild Flowers*. Writing to his brother Isaac in May, 1806, Bloomfield told him of announcing *Wild Flowers*, sent him a copy, and sent with it another sure sign of his current popularity.

The engravers J. Storer and J. Greig, who had previously published books of illustrations of the works and regions of both Cowper and Burns, chose Bloomfield from the living authors of his era to include in their series. The poet was able to send his brother a copy of the ponderously titled *Views in Suffolk, Norfolk, and Northhamptonshire; Illustrative of the Works of Robert Bloomfield; Accompanied with Descriptions: to which is Annexed, a Memoir of the Poet's Life by E[dward] W[edlake] Brayley.*

In the summer of 1807, Bloomfield was again plagued with too much work and too many interruptions. Sick in mind and hence in body, he found that even his crafting of aeolian harps was slowed as he suffered "the unseasonable and impudand [*sic*] visits of the vain,

and the interested, and the curious, taking up my time, inviting me
to dinner, etc. etc." (MS 28,268, 230). The pressures of too little
money and of time wasted in dunning his customers brought a
recurrence of his nightmares—bad dreams "that would appall [*sic*]
the Devil" (MS 28,268, 230). Perhaps to escape the pains of that
summer on City Road, perhaps to enjoy the company of friends and
the English countryside, Bloomfield accepted the invitation of Mr.
and Mrs. T. J. Lloyd Baker and their friends to accompany them on
a tour along the river Wye. In August, he was with the party at
Stout's Hill and writing to his wife of the charming valley of Uley. If
the city had affected Bloomfield's creative urge, his journey to the
country was to restore it. After the first five days, he wrote of his joy:
"[T]his morning [we] engaged an Old Welshman with a cart with
benches, and three little horses, to carry us to the summit of the
Sugar-loaf Mountain, such fun, such a road, and such a feast on the
mountain moss, and such a sight! I shall talk of it all the rest of my
life" (*C*, 46). After a few days' rest at Stout's Hill, Bloomfield was
ready to return home and told his wife, "I shall have an interesting
journal to exhibit on my return, and a thousand things to explain"
(*C*, 47). Both the journal and an account in poetry he had intended
for the general fun of the party and of his family, but his excitement
and the new images of England would not release him for years. The
trip and the friendships it intensified began a new course for
Bloomfield's correspondence. To the Bakers with whom he had
shared the experience and to Miss Sharp, Mrs. Baker's sister, the
poet wrote with great intensity for the next few years.

While his friends had sketched those scenes which were most
appealing to them, Bloomfield converted the rural images into
verbal ones. Then in November, 1807, Bloomfield agreed to exchange his journal for the sketches Mrs. Baker had made, sketches
he planned to try his hand at copying. That winter—a period during
which his writing frequently stopped—Bloomfield laboriously
copied the sketches and enlarged his poetical journal. Amused with
the pictures he produced, he wrote to Mr. Baker that he pleased
himself but found his trees "amazingly like a pile of Chesshire
Cheeses. And one in particular, I was hampered with, it seem'd to
have a determination to resemble a large Pil Jar with a handle, but I
cut the handle off, and it became as good a tree as the rest, aye, and
as good as some that I have seen at Sadler's Wells" (MS 28,268,
245).

In mid-January Bloomfield told Mrs. Baker of seven hundred

lines of poetry which advanced the history of the tour to Sugar-loaf where he was moved to evoke the spirit of Burns. He returned her sketches and sent with them his prose journal which he then found too full of personal talk to be of general interest (MS 28,268, 249v). February found him still revising lines and being drawn for the militia. Following the custom for older men called into service, he extricated himself for the considerable sum of twenty pounds. (MS 28,268, 252v).

Still working in April, he wrote to Mrs. Baker of his slow progress. With eleven hundred lines he was only one-third finished. Questioning again the value of the work to any save the party of travelers, he insisted, "but I must go on, to get rid of the impressions, that can by no other means be worn out" (MS 28,268, 255).

Further work was interrupted during the summer of 1808 by the preparation of a preface for the stereotype edition of his work. In a difficult summer for body and spirit, Bloomfield found relief only in rambling out from the city to recall the last summer's journey. "Blessings on the recollections of that Tour!" he wrote. "It cheers me like a dram of whisky or a Mug of Welch ale" (MS 28,268, 258r). The return of his ill health elicited the admission in December that he had not "budg'd an inch after the Muses since April, but I have a strong notion that we shall be friends in the Spring" (MS 28,268, 261r–v).

Bloomfield's memories of rural life were considerably stirred in the fall when his eldest daughter, Hannah, visited Mr. Austin's farm and walked the roads and fields of her father's youth, and he wrote to her that he was happily at work on his Wye poem. Despite a recurrence of his rheumatic affliction, he had his "old dreams strengthened rather than diminished" (MS 28,268, 273–75v).

A thought that followed Bloomfield for some time as he worked on the journal found expression in January, 1811, as he wrote to Mrs. Baker that he had become convinced that it was fit for publication. He had offered it to his bookseller. After finishing it according to his first plan and showing it to Mr. Inskip, himself a poet, and to Mr. Weston, Bloomfield set about a careful revision. "I conceived that it was, owing to the careless and hasty manner of its early composition, much too Hudibrastic, and contained a vast deal of useless matter, which might give way to the superior graces of nature, or to unbridled fancy" (*C*, 50). The poem, even in its "ruder state," was praised by Samuel Rogers, who thought it would be a success if published. So Bloomfield, revising and writing out the whole of it three times, "gave the brat a name" and proceeded with his plans to publish.

The "Journal," now divided into four books and interspersed with "incidental ballads," was to be published with only four plates, the expense of which the publishers first thought to minimize by using several of Bloomfield's own sketches. The poet was relieved, finally, to ask Robert Bransby Cooper, of the original party, to do the drawings (C, 50–52).

It was August, 1811, however, before Bloomfield could send Mrs. Baker one of the early copies of the book now entitled *The Banks of the Wye: A Poem.* The poet dedicated the book to his companions on the journey, the Bakers, Mr. Cooper, and Cooper's family. To Mrs. Baker he wrote, "Read my verses, and travel with me over again; my heart will be in perfect unison. There are several passages entirely new to you, and some which I think you will like; but remember that you are a critic, and have a right (I suppose as great as any of them) to say what you please of it" (C, 53).

VIII   *Distress and Decline*

Bloomfield's happiness at having done with *The Banks of the Wye* was countered by two other events of 1811—two deaths which would put in ruin whatever chance for solvency the poet might have had. The first was that of the old duke of Grafton, Augustus Henry Fitzroy, Bloomfield's first great patron. The duke was succeeded by his son the most noble duke of Grafton, right honorable earl of Euston, Lord Charles Fitzroy, M.P., who had less than his father's interest in shoemaker-poets. After Lofft had a letter from the new duke stating that the poet need only write and state the amount of the annuity, Bloomfield wrote to the new duke reminding him of the fifteen pounds per annum due at the time of the duke's death (C, 53).

The second unhappy event was the death in August of Mr. Hood, the more active partner in the bookselling concern. The business came into the hands of Mr. Sharp, a younger partner. Bloomfield was pleased for a time with his dealings with Sharp, and the first edition of *The Banks of the Wye* was selling at a good rate. But just as it appeared that a second edition would be called for, a bookseller returned five hundred copies which were redistributed for selling before any new edition was made. In April, 1812, when Bloomfield called to exchange agreements for *The Banks of the Wye*, he found the near-bankrupt Sharp quitting the business. With excited expectations the poet noted that Sharp had sold his quarter of Bloomfield's books to a bookseller named Crosby for 509 pounds. "And, consequently, if such copyrights as his, all in a few years coming back into my own hands, will fetch that price, what is the worth of my entire half, and the other reverting half? Certainly not less than £2,000" (C, 54). Ironically, such expectations, although never fulfilled, would tantalize the poet in his last years, sometimes commanding him to live on when he felt he might die.

"The black side of the story," which Bloomfield heard the same day, was that Sharp had also sold 4,500 of the poet's books, given two to three years' credit for them, and was unable or unwilling to advance any money on their sale (C, 54). Already living on the whole of his income, Bloomfield decided to move his family to the country where cheaper lodgings and a living generally less expensive could be had. On April 7, 1812, the day after discovering Sharp's activities, he wrote again to remind the new duke of Grafton of his own and Lofft's petitions for the annuity. There is a tone of harried desperation in the letter: "I would not thus intrude now, had I not determined to live in the country and actually sent my goods and wife and five children to Shefford in Bedfordshire, for I find the expenses of London housekeeping too heavy for my precarious income, and have besides by no means good health" (C, 54). The retirement that many eighteenth-century writers sought and in which Bloomfield might have otherwise have delighted was forced upon him by the city and its finances.

In May he wrote to Mrs. Baker that the present duke would continue the annuity of fifteen pounds, which would in effect allow him to live rent free. He was pleased with the country around him and with his house and middling garden, but the "poetical revolution" that followed the death of Mr. Hood still plagued him (MS 28,268, 322r–v). Although his expenses in Shefford were considerably reduced, by September he was about to borrow forty pounds for six months from Mr. Baker.

Business drew the poet back to London in October, and he wrote home to his daughter Hannah with great bitterness. He had drawn some money on Crosby, the bookseller, and had found that *The Wye* sold well. Another edition would be wanted, and yet he wrote:

I never yet was half so disgusted with London. If my health and spirits were not so greatly amended by living in the country, and by overcoming the horrible and destroying grief which I suffer from domestic troubles, I should certainly sink under my load, and rashly sell my property in the books, and forswear London for ever.

God bless you all.

Your cheated and bamboozled Father

Robert Bloomfield. (C, 55)

There may be a hint of his old humor in the close, and certainly a part of it was with him the following April (1813) when he returned to the city to see the reviews of his new and revised *Wye* and to arrange for reprinting the stereotype edition. In a coffeehouse he drafted his letter "To Whom it may Concern," and after gossip of his brother Nathaniel whose family was afflicted with grave illness, he jibed, "I can write only as Rabbits S——t, in little bits, for the cart wheels roar, and the waiters are noisy, and there is a chimney on fire within sight, and a brave crowd.——" There was some consolation in the trip, however, for he saw his old friend Dyer (MS 28,268, 330–31).

In May he wrote to his wife from the city. Although some sights amused him, he had lost his relish for the theater and had not attended. A cobbler, he found, now lived in their old workshop, and his prices were terribly high. More significant than these desultory thoughts, however, is his mention of renewed writing, a piece called "Jennet" or probably "Alfred and Jennet" as it later appeared in *May Day with the Muses* (MS 28, 268, 332–33).

In the summer and fall of 1813, the poet was in further "pecuniary difficulties" and in poor health. There was some danger that the whole of his affairs would go into litigation, and his resulting disgust may have complicated his physical ills. He suffered a great deal of tension and had been advised by the doctor to slam the doors to relieve it. But the wind, he claimed, always managed to slam them first. Now, he felt, he must live until March for his family's sake and cheat the booksellers by living until his copyrights reverted to him. For that he would live, "if not to dig in the earth for my lost muse" (MS 28,268, 334r).

Early in 1814, Bloomfield was again in London attempting to wrest his copyrights for *The Farmer's Boy* from Crosby and presenting a few more papers to Longmans, whom he felt to be his allies in legal matters. Of Crosby he wrote, "He shall not vex my pretty little sleek, mouse-backed spirit for fourteen years to come, rest assured of that" (C, 56).[31] Bloomfield's spirits sank lower when he caught cold after a lengthy wait in a drafty printer's office and missed a party with Samuel Rogers (MS 28,268, 336).

Soon, the poet left the city for a visit to Dover where he watched the landing of Count Metternich and the king (MS 28,268, 340–43v), and was at home in Shefford for the celebration of peace in July. Bloomfield, however, had no summer of pastoral calm, for he buried his daughter Mary Anne and fretted again with his finances. Of the others in his family, Bloomfield wrote to Mr. Baker in the fall of 1814:

My wife is a staunch disciple of Johanna [*sic*] Southcott,[32] my four children at home. The eldest boy [Charles], formerly lame, is growing and healthy, and is making a rapid progress in arithmetic. My youngest boy [Robert] is seven and a half, and likewise goes to school. My eldest girl [Hannah] is a woman in years, and, I hope, in all that may continue her my friend. The youngest girl [Charlotte] is thirteen, and is growing very fast. (*C*, 58)

Of his progress at poetry he wrote:

You would probably, if you saw me, enquire if my mind was still running on new subjects for the Muse? I can give you little satisfaction on that subject, but I sometimes dream that I shall one day venture again before the public, in my old manner, some Country tales, and spiced with love and courtship might yet please, for Rural life by the art of Cooking may be made a relishing and highly flavor'd dish, whatever it may be in reality. (MS 28,268, 351)

Although he sounded dejected and now wrote with spectacles and wore a wig, he could sign himself, "with these double eyes, and a heart that cannot loose its old impressions."

The next years added more troubles to Bloomfield's already taxing lot, for it was necessary to place his children in whatever employment he could find for them. Of all his expectations which were dashed, not being better able to help his family seemed to cause his greatest anguish. In the fall of 1815, plans were made to bind Charles as apprentice to a Mr. Adams and to find Charlotte a place as a milliner. Hampered in the correspondence necessary for this effort by failing eyesight and hard pressed by debt, Bloomfield nevertheless resolved not to be worn down (MS 28,268, 356).

Some relief might have come when *Rural Tales* reverted to him in January, but in November, 1815, he doubted that he could sell it.

The whole city, in fact, seemed to share his financial woes, and he remarked that "this is what we get by thumping the French" (MS 28,268, 356r).

Even the publication that year of his children's tale, *The History of Little Davy's New Hat*, did not appear to remove any of the financial pressure from the Bloomfields. In December, 1815, Robert wrote to his daughter that the whole town knew that he would have to move yet another time to a lesser house (MS 28,268, 359r). He was distressed that the move might make Hannah uncomfortable, and he urged her in a kind, sad fashion to learn some work she could live from.

Bloomfield's complaints, rheumatism, an inflamed leg, and a great sickness in the stomach, returned in 1816 (MS 28,268, 362v). His financial distress was so acute that in September Sir Samuel Egerton Brydges and other of his supporters issued a subscription in his behalf in an effort to purchase for him an annuity. The appeal was directed "To the Friends and Admirers of Robert Bloomfield:"

Several noblemen and gentlemen of Suffolk, the patrons and friends of Robert Bloomfield, a native of that county, so well known as a pastoral poet by his "Farmer's Boy" and other compositions, which have confirmed on him the fame of pure and native genius, having been informed that he is now labouring under embarrassment, owing partly to the failure of his former booksellers, having entered into a subscription to be applied in the purchase of an annuity, which may secure independence and comfort to himself and his family during the remainder of his own sickly existence, the literary friends of this amiable poet are exerting themselves to procure contributions to this benevolent design. And one who admires the moral worth of his character, as well as his writings, is willing to contribute his share of active friendship on this occasion, by thus soliciting the notice of those among whom this paper is circulated, to a case where they may bestow the most substantial benefits on an individual whose productions have given genuine and enlightened pleasure to every reader of sensibility, taste, and virtue. At the head of the subscription in Suffolk are the Duke of Norfolk, the Duke of Grafton, the Earl of Bristol, Lord Rous, the County Members, &c., &c. (*C*, 58).

There followed directions as to where the gifts might be paid.

It is difficult to ascertain the effectiveness of the appeal. It seems to have drawn more notice than money. When in November Bloomfield wrote to Hannah, now at Miss Weston's Drapery in Twickenham, the fund had attracted 120 pounds in Suffolk and twenty pounds in Kent (MS 28,268, 364v). Such an amount would hardly produce enough income for any man's lifetime support. In December, 1816, shortly after his fiftieth birthday, the poet wrote again to his daughter. His neighbors' gossip seemed not to amuse him as it once did, and he had found no place for young Robert. Of the public efforts in his behalf he quipped, "The Subscription—Aye, the Subscription goes on very much like a Donkey in a dirt lane with his legs tied" (MS 28,268, 366v). He was thankful, though, for what little it brought him and for the dozen bottles of port a patron sent. Suddenly, before closing with remarks on the general good health of all the family, he wrote, "I see no reviews, no papers, but *Hunt* and the mild moderate *Cobbet*—I feel lost—" (MS 28,268, 367).

By February, 1817, with a second edition of *Davy* at press and a bit of money in his hand, he was more cheerful and able to send a few pounds to his daughter. He had applied to the duke of Grafton, who was in arrears with his annuity, and the duke had complied by paying it. But, as Mr. Unwin has already indicated,[33] the duke's reply was most chilly in regretting that "Mr. B.'s muse should have been so long silent." The duke went on to describe the fall of one of the largest trees in neighboring Salcey Forest, an event which, had Bloomfield's muse witnessed it, "might have roused her from her lethargy" (C, 59). The incident later became the basis for the "Forester's Song" in Bloomfield's last volume of poetry.[34]

During the summer and fall of 1817, Bloomfield attempted to place his son Charles in a position as schoolmaster, and it may have been his success at this endeavor and the achievements of his other children which caused him to write that winter, "I feel a placid composure of soul, a kind of sunshine holiday of the soul which I have not felt for two years past; I have paid all my principal debts, and have the Duke's allowance now due. . . . In the mean time I am persuing [*sic*] my old theme with all my powers" (MS 28,268, 384r-v). The writing he referred to became *May Day with the Muses*, part of which he had begun years before.

IX *A Final Book of Verse*

It was the spring of 1819, however, before another mention of progress with his poetry appears in Bloomfield's letters. At that point, he wrote to Samuel Rogers to negotiate a draft on the capital of a part of his subscription, assuring Rogers that "I have not forgotten to help myself": "I have composed nearly a thousand lines of a new work. . . . A part of these I have sent to the Duke of

Grafton, and have his reply in a style which is flattering and consolatory even to a poet. This work, if it pleases God to continue my health, will be finished by next Michaelmas, and no pecuniary considerations shall throw it out of my hands until it is done" (C, 61). For as long as it lasted, writing, and successful writing most notably, spelled an end to Bloomfield's physical and mental complaints. Then Bloomfield heard that the publisher, Murray, had given "Parson Crabbe" three thousand pounds for his *Tales* (MS 28,268, 399r–v). Evidently hoping to find his fortune with Crabbe's publisher, Bloomfield was a little disappointed when it appeared that his own publishers, Baldwin, Cradock, and Joy, would publish the work immediately. There are a number of indications that his great hopes, his expectations, were against his own better judgment controlling him again.

It may have been that Bloomfield's hopes led him to demand too much, for on September 17, he wrote to Hannah that he would flee out to Windsor for a few days to loose his "bag of blue Devils." Baldwin had been cold, and the poet had small faith in his own efforts through his friends Park and Samuel Rogers to place the poem with Murray. What Bloomfield would not believe was that he and his poetry could be "out of fashion from the taste of the times" (MS 28,268, 404). Typically, his great concern was with disappointing his family.

It was not until May, 1820, that Bloomfield again corresponded concerning the manuscript, and it was to Murray that his urgent letter was addressed. Of all of his letters, it is here that he comes closest to abandoning his dignity:

In consequence of a letter from my good friend T. Park, Esq., of Hampstead, I send you a MS poem for your perusal, and particularly request that you will read it *through*. I must presume that you know my origin, my history, and the success of my former publications.

My wish is to dispose of this if anyone deem it worth his while to take it off my hands.

If, sir, you will put me out of my suspense as soon as possible, you will greatly add to the quiet of my own mind, and to the character I have always heard of your generous conduct as a publisher. (C, 62)

Murray's reply was negative. The poet's frustration in attempting to publish *May Day* was not his only difficulty in the next year. His old friend and companion on the trip down the Wye, Thomas Baker, wrote in May, 1821, to tell Bloomfield of rumors which might cost the poet the favor of his public and his patrons. The reports had it that Bloomfield did not go to church, that he opposed the government, and that he read the wrong magazines. Baker hoped to elicit a denial that would help to remove this pall and stop the patrons who were quitting what they now thought to be a dangerous man both "Deistical and Republican" in spirit (MS 28,268, 415–16).

What Bloomfield seemed to hear best was Baker's mention of patrons withdrawing their accustomed support, for his first bitter question asked from whom, other than the duke of Grafton, he was accustomed to having support? Remembering his early vow never to speak or write on those two grand topics, religion and politics, which "keep the world in agitation," the poet protested that he had been surrounded by Catholics, Deists, Quakers, Unitarians, Methodists, Calvinists, and in the end he felt himself as good as any of them. The problem, he thought, lay in his little town where the people had so little business to keep that they gossiped and started troublesome rumors (MS 28,268, 417r–v).

Baker returned Bloomfield's letter with a note again pleading for a statement that he was not hostile to church or state and that he kept no evil company (MS 28,268, 418). The poet's reply reveals more the nature of the man than anything he could deny or admit.

Abandoning his resolution to be silent, Bloomfield explained two instances which might have given rise to the criticism. In the first case his connection had been with a Deist friend of Capel Lofft's. Bloomfield had known him for a short time during the early years in London, but found an inconsistency in keeping company with the man and dropped him. Then came people of all predilections including some Unitarians who without the poet's knowledge had written to the duke of Grafton intimating that Bloomfield would make "a pretty little Unitarian" (MS 28,268, 421r–v). Since the duke himself had attended their services, it seemed natural that the poet in truckling to his patron might do so too. The duke, however, expressed his wish to exert no influence over Bloomfield, who was left to conclude that since he himself could give no money to the Unitarian cause, they must simply have been seeking proselytes.

Bloomfield went on to enumerate other false rumors that had plagued his career including an assertion by Cobbett that he had been taken in tow by the government to prevent him from writing in favor of the people. There followed a most direct statement in answer to the rumors: "But to the point.—I say then there is not a Man or woman living who would or could say to *my face* that I have

renounced the doctrines of Christ, or his Miracles.—There is not a
soul upon earth to say 'you are an enemy to the Government of your
Country.' Fools, cannot they see that the form of Government of a
Country is rather different to the administration?" (MS 28,268,
421r–v). On June 1, 1821, Bloomfield sent a postscript on the
subject, hoping that it could then sleep forever.[35]

By October, his last book of poems was at the engravers, and he
knew little of its slow progress. A possible result of the long delay in
printing the book and winning some income was the unhappy
necessity of selling the old family cottage. Had his mother left a
shilling with a hole in it or an old cat, he would have kept them. But
a house ate more than a cat and was more than he could afford to
keep (MS 28,268, 426–27). In Wickett's reconstruction of the trans-
action, there is yet another irony. A questionable title to the
property in the end prevented Bloomfield from receiving so much
as a sixpence.[36]

May Day with the Muses, which appeared in 1822, was at least a
moderate success, and a second edition was called for the same year.
In the preface Bloomfield wrote, "I have been reported to be dead;
but I can assure the reader that this, like many other reports, is not
true. I have written these tales in anxiety, and in a wretched state of
health; and if these formidable foes have not incapacitated me, but
left me free to meet the public eye with any degree of credit, that
degree of credit I am sure I shall gain. I am, with remembrance of
what is past, Most respectfully, Robert Bloomfield."[37] This last
seems less a sloppy bit of nostalgia than a recognition that his tales
would be read by old friends, not a new public. The reference to
other untrue reports was, it appears, his only public refutation of the
charges against him about which Lloyd Baker had written.

For Bloomfield, a more pleasant interlude in the spring and
summer of 1822 came with his acquaintance with the works of John
Clare. Clare had known of Bloomfield for many years, having
Bloomfield's *Wild Flowers* in his library in his twenty-first year.[38]
The shoemaker-poet was a great favorite of Clare's and he evidently
asked that Edward Drury, a cousin of his publisher, send
Bloomfield a copy of *Poems Descriptive of Rural Life and Scenery*.
In a letter to Clare, Bloomfield responded to the poetry of his
"Brother Bard, and fellow labourer":

Some weeks past Mr. Drury of Stamford sent me your Voll^m. and I have
only been prevented from answering by ill health, which began in January

and seems to threaten a long continuance. I am however very glad to have lived to see your poems: They have given me and my family an uncommon pleasure, and they will have the same effect on all kindred minds and that's enough; for, as for writing rhimes for Clods and sticks and expecting them to read them, I have never found any fun in that in all my life, and I have past your age 26 years. I am delighted with your "address to the Lark," "Summer Morning," and "Evening" &c. &c. In fact I had better not turn critic in my first letter, but say the truth, that nothing upon the great theatre of what is call'd the world (our English world) can give me half the pleasure I feel at seeing a man start up from the humble walks of life and show himself to be what I think you are.—What that is, ask a higher power,—for though learning is not to be contemn'd it did not give you this. I must write to Mr. Drury, and Mr. Claydon, but not now.—I am far from well—have just been walking amidst the most luxuriant crops with my eldest Daughter and two Sons, but find myself tired.

Let nothing prevent you from writing, for though I cannot further your interest I can feel an interest in it, and I assure you I do.

I am *heartily* tired (not of my subject) and must beg you to accept my congratulations and my wishes for your health, which I find after all is one of the most essential blessings of life. [39]

Bloomfield's postscript informed Clare, "I have written this on 'my Old Oak Table,' and I think you know what I mean?" It was his writing table celebrated earlier in verse, which he had kept with him for years.

On May 3, Bloomfield sent a copy of *May Day* to Clare with a note that began, "Neighbor John:"

If we were still nearer neighbors I would see you, & thank you personally for the two Volumes of your Poems sent me so long ago. I write with such labour and difficulty that I cannot venture to praise or discriminate like a critic, but must only say that you have given us great pleasure.

I beg your acceptance of my just published little Volume; and, sick & ill as I continually feel, I can join with you heartily in your exclamation.
What is life? [40]

X   *Last Attempts*

Bloomfield visited London again in the fall, and a letter to his son Charles reveals a continuing interest in the book trade. In the correspondence of these late years his remarks on the financial success of other authors stand alone with no reference to his own plight. Whether it was bitterness or hope which led him to comment in the first place, is difficult to judge, but the rest of his tone in such letters is even, sometimes humorous. His chief concern continued to be his children, their careers, and their knowledge of the world. His advice was gentle, and he carefully avoided the dreadful pressure a parent's high expectations might have put upon them.

In October, his sons visited with him in Shefford. Through all of the poet's fifty-six years family ties had been of great importance and in this last year of his life, they were no less so. The departure of his sons gnawed at him. Several weeks, in fact, were required before the emotional pain was lessened (MS 28,268, 430). There was one project with Charles, however, which continued to bring Bloomfield great pleasure. Both father and son were working on a children's book composed of letters ostensibly written by "winged and creeping correspondents"[41] and translated by the Bloomfields. Eventually entitled "The Bird and Insect's Post-Office," the work was first printed in Bloomfield's *Remains* in 1823.[42]

This second attempt at a children's book was to teach children something of natural history with a "correspondence between different beasts and insects upon topics connected with their habits and feelings" (MS 28,268, 121–22). Bloomfield thought his children might compose it with what knowledge of nature they had drawn from books or observation. The project so interested Charles in literary endeavors that he also began to test his skill at "poetical pieces" as his father called them (MS 28,268, 432).

Bloomfield may have intended to publish this joint composition with some bits of poetry by himself and Charles, for he urged his son to send him the manuscript so that he might show it to Mr. Harvey by Christmas (presumably Harvey of Harvey and Darton who published *Little Davy*). On December 23, 1822, while Bloomfield was expecting some of Charles' poetry in the mail, he wrote that he himself would "continue with 'Gosling John' as fast as I can and try to keep my spirits up, and to reckon upon another season or two of existence at least, when my affairs, I think, will mend themselves" (MS 28,268, 432r–v). The optimism about his affairs was ill founded; what optimism he felt about his health was prompted by the absence for some time of his painful stomach attacks. "Gosling John" was a character in the poet's village drama *Hazelwood Hall*, which the period of good health allowed him to compose.

Bloomfield had begun *Hazelwood Hall: A Village Drama* some years before. In 1802, he wrote to his brother George:

Your observations on the possibility of my composing a pastoral drama, and your hints as to proper materials, &c., are extremely interesting. Mr. Shield suggested that something of the sort might be done. You have awakened the wish rather than the hope of ever succeeding in that line. What do I know of *Stage effect?* Nevertheless, I have no doubt but I could tie a story together that should speak my own sentiments and feelings, and of course you would like to see it. You are, I know well, aware of how much depends on *choice of subject.* (*C*, 29)

In April, 1823, he wrote further of the course of composition:

This little dramatic sketch is not so new as it may appear to be. So long ago as the year 1805, a gentleman met me on the sands at Worthing, and asked me to his house, &c. but I never saw him afterwards. He gave his address, "Mr. Goldhawk, Hazelwood-Hall, Leith-Hill, Surrey." The names never left my mind, and I then thought of trying them in a village tale, or drama, which I actually began. The subject has slept ever since, until the publication of my "May Day," last spring, left me leisure and inclination to put it into its present form.[43]

It is apparent here that Bloomfield's last productions are (as was *Little Davy* in 1815) largely the ends of works begun in his most productive period. This is not to say, however, that after 1811 he could produce nothing new. Revisions, emendations, and enlargements are surely a part of an artist's enterprise. The considerable revisions of his *Wye*, the composition of *May Day with the Muses,* and these other, perhaps lesser productions are worthy considerations for those who find his later years empty, wasted, or full of "an effete but genteel artiness."[44]

The nightmares, the headaches, the stomach complaints, the failing eyesight and more added to the tensions of Bloomfield's financially pressed last years. He found himself distracted and experienced lapses of memory. But his resulting melancholia must be carefully weighed against his continuing love for his work and family and his humor and whimsey, which show him far too strong and competent to be the object of indiscriminate pity. Unfortunately, even Wickett's biography, which does attempt to correct the history of Bloomfield's last years, fails to bring the history to balance. Quoting from a letter to George Bloomfield written in February, 1823, Wickett sees only the "confused and troubled state of his mind":

But one great cause for my writing now is, that for about a fortnight now I have tried to break from my violent dreams in a morning and for myself to believe that my Elder Brother is Living! And then Isaac comes across my mind, but though I know him to be dead his image is so fresh in my memory as yours. It is a strange feeling and I don't much like it and I wish particularly you would let me see your own handwriting to dispel the illusion, and pull the wool out of my brain, for I am afraid I have been working too hard lately. I know very well there are a wife and bairns living in Well Street, but I cannot find you nor bring you living before my mind's eye. But the mind's eye is sometimes misty—pray write directly. My health is tolerably firm and steady. Honington I have done with, and it seems effectually to have done with me, for the devil a farthing of money can I get in my hour of necessity for all the horrible expense and cost I have sustained.

Love to Susan and the Bits
Yours as ever Robert Bloomfield.

P.S. Writing is to me harder than digging was 40 years ago, but my mind, my power of Composition, is as strong and more active than ever it was in my life.[45]

The mental confusion is obvious, the phenomenon not uncommon to persons in failing health or advanced years. What is most notable, however, is Bloomfield's recognition of the hallucination, his determination to control it, and his sense of perspective. The courage of the postscript and the balanced remark about his health cannot be ignored. The claim by early biographers that he died after years of mental and physical turmoil during which doctors feared for his sanity is simply not supported by his letters. Too, the strong evidence of his continuing labors creates a very different picture. Any general collapse could have come only in the very last months of his life. He was working, and continued to do so. His spirit was troubled but not defeated. He was living into his death.

By May, Bloomfield had sent *Hazelwood Hall* to Baldwin and was anxiously awaiting that gentleman's reply. In the last of his letters in the British Library collection, mention of the book is surrounded with more of the gentle advice with which he guided his children. The letter, from May 2, 1823, was written in fine weather and found the poet as well as he thought he would ever be. To Charles he recommended buying what clothes would best improve his appearance and perhaps enhance his stature as a schoolmaster. Admitting that it was difficult to neglect appearances with social impunity, he commented, "Appearance is not everything, but it has more power than it is worth, and perhaps than it ought" (MS 28,268, 434).

Bloomfield, then, three months before his death at fifty-seven, was in moderately good health and surprisingly high spirits. He was still curious about the world and involved in his own work: he announced that the family had been reading in the memoirs of Napoleon at St. Helena and that he still wrote at the "Post Office" (MS 28,268, 434v–35).

On August 19, 1823, attended by his faithful oldest daughter Hannah, Robert Bloomfield died. His remains were taken from the simple house on Bedford Street in Shefford to the country churchyard at Campton, Bedfordshire. The inscription on the headstone says, "Let His Wild Native Wood Notes Tell the Rest."

XI   *Retrospect*

Bloomfield's death, like any person's, left much unspoken, much unfinished. His "Post Office" was not printed until Joseph Weston edited the *Remains* in 1824 for the benefit of the family. The meeting that he and Clare had hoped for never came. Clare wrote to their mutual friend Thomas Inskip:

Poor Bloomfield I deeply regret now its too late I had made up my resolution to see him this summer but if he had been alive I should have been disappointed by this coldblooded lethargy of a disease what it is I cannot tell it even affects my senses very much by times—I heard of Bloomfield's death and it shockd my feelings poor fellow you say right when you exclaim 'who would be a poet' I sincerely lovd the man and I admire his genius and readily (nay gladly) acknowledge his superiority as a Poet.[46]

Bloomfield's intense desire to provide security for his family also remained unfulfilled and his literary reputation, which might yet have been salvaged, was subjected to a vicious attack in the *Monthly Magazine* in September, 1823. It was left to Joseph Weston to mount an urgent defense on both fronts by rushing to edit the *Remains* in which he chastised the *Monthly's* reviewer.

Some comment is due on the general nature of Bloomfield, this surprising man. He was, first, gentle but not lacking in spirit and independence; he was not the drab, whining, defenseless soul envisioned by some Victorian preface writers. He was as complex a man as any biographer could wish for, yet he was not blessed with a scandal-filled life that might have given him greater notoriety. Imprudent in his generosity or liberality and cursed with a courageous optimism which produced "great expectations," Bloomfield fed his own melancholia through these normally positive traits. In all, his periods of anxiety and the bad dreams which frequently accompanied them were balanced, often interspersed, with demonstrations of a keen sense of irony, a wry wit, and a quiet acceptance of paradox.

Bloomfield's awareness of literature, music, and the mechanics of publishing has already been recounted. In the *Remains* are some records of his other interests. He researched and composed a pamphlet, "Nature's Music," on the history and construction of aeolian harps.[47] His other studies, of enclosure, garden spiders, Stonehenge, astronomy and Egyptian architecture, the discovery of mammoth skeletons in America, and a hundred other topics, reveal a restless, curious mind.

Among his passions, that for his family may have been strongest. Throughout his letters, however, runs the constant theme of love for the country and for the rural folk and traditions which he knew. His distaste for city life was evident, although the theater, the magazines, and the galleries all pleased him. He could take great pride in his city-learned trade of shoemaking with its history of famous exponents, but thought such city workers more vulgar and ignorant than their peers in the country (MS 28,268, 435). When he once indicated that he felt himself at home in the city, he wrote, "I ought to have said that I wish'd the Country my home; and that radical first-planted principle in my composition can never be blotted out by London and all it can produce."[48] The meaning of this antiurban spirit for Bloomfield's art will be seen in the following chapters, but it is important here as a final note to his biography. He was aware, I think fully aware, that urbanization threatened to end those traditions from which he drew his identity and the energy of his art. His religion and his very soul, perhaps like those of countless of his countrymen forced into London by enclosure and economic change, were rooted in the half-pagan, half-Christian soil of the country. His small skepticism and a great wisdom grew, I think, from there. His daughter Hannah once took from his pocket a scrap of his own verse occasioned by May Day night of 1822 and the recent publication of his *May Day with the Muses,* which may best illuminate his passion:

> It is the voice thou gavest me, God of Love
> And all I see & feel still bears thy sway
> And when the Spring breaks forth in mead & grove
> Thou art my God, thou art the God of May.[49]

CHAPTER 2

The Farmer's Boy: *Openness, Closure, and Limitations within the Natural Order*

I Critical and Popular Reception

IT is on *The Farmer's Boy; A Rural Poem* that Robert Bloomfield's career was built, and on it rests the last vestiges of his reputation. In terms of popularity alone, it was an astounding success,[1] and, although its critical reception was mixed it did please Coleridge, Wordsworth, Hazlitt, Rogers, Dyer, and a host of others.

Southey reviewed the poem enthusiastically in *The Critical Review*, declaring that Bloomfield had the "eye and feeling of a poet" and had written an excellent work that "abounds with beautiful lines of accurate and minute description."[2] Olleyett Woodhouse in the *Monthly Review or Literary Journal* claimed that Bloomfield's poetical skill elevated his humble subject matter with success far beyond what could be expected from an "uncultivated mind" and asserted that the shoemaker poet shared with Thomson "a musical ear, flowing numbers, feeling, piety, poetic imagery and animation, a taste for the picturesque, a true sense of the natural and pathetic, force of thought, and liveliness of imagination."[3] Enthusiastic and sympathetic notice of *The Farmer's Boy* also appeared in *The Lady's Monthly Museum* (August, 1800) and that journal began to follow Bloomfield's career closely. Another of the inevitable comparisons with Thomson appeared in *The Monthly Mirror* (March, 1800) which found Bloomfield's poem delightful, rivaling *The Seasons* in some respects. Coleridge in a letter to James Webbe Tobin wrote, "What W[ordsworth] and I have seen of the *Farmer's Boy* (only a few short extracts) pleased us very much."[4] Later, he planned a positive critical statement of his own. In his *Lectures on the English Poets*, Hazlitt would find many merits in the poem, while Nathan Drake in *Literary Hours* extravagantly claimed that the poem was

54

the best pastoral "since the days of Theocritus."[5] George Dyer, highly pleased with a copy of the poem sent to him by Lofft, responded at length:

Yes Sir, I have read *The Farmer's Boy*, and intend to read it over and over again some time hence. The Farmer's Boy appears to me a truly original and beautiful poem. It recalled to my mind those ages and those countries in which the poet and the shepherd were more naturally united, and under those circumstances some of the earliest Scotch Ballads were written, and they please us because they breathe the language of nature and speak to the heart. . . . I perceive no fopperies—no meretricious ornaments, no language of bigotry and enthusiasm in Bloomfield.[6]

The poem influenced David Service whose title characters in *The Caledonian Herd Boy* (1802) and *Crispin, or the Apprentice Boy* (1804) owe much in conception to Bloomfield's Giles, and soon Ewan Clark followed with *The Rustic* (1805), "another attempt to outdo Bloomfield."[7] Too, W. H. Ireland, the fabricator of Shakespeare papers, shows the influence of Bloomfield in *The Sailor Boy* (1809).[8] John Clare, whose warm praise of Bloomfield has already been recounted, was also influenced by Bloomfield in his *Shepherd's Calendar*.[9] In its time, then, *The Farmer's Boy* enjoyed a wide popularity, considerable critical acclaim, and a modest influence over other poets. Most important is the popularity. Although *The Farmer's Boy* is part of a well established tradition of country poems—a tradition including works not only by Theocritus, Hesiod, Thomson, and Goldsmith, but also by Gray, Cowper, Dyer, and many others—few had its extraordinary impact on such a huge and varied audience. Mere popular appeal does not, of course, necessarily equate with literary influence on major writers. But it can revitalize a tradition and indicate clearly to other writers the extent of the audience that would welcome rural subjects.

It should be helpful to examine the structure, style, and thematic character of *The Farmer's Boy* for those literary qualities which explain at least a portion of the poem's popularity and its merit. Although Bloomfield's limitations in education and experience were generally those of the "peasant poet," what he accomplished within his inventive bounds is of impressive quality. His artistic accomplishment in *The Farmer's Boy*, in fact, is underscored by the paradox of his wise acceptance of those limitations and his simultaneous struggle to overcome them.

II   *Structuring the Poem: Openness, Closure, and Limitations*

Several rather obvious, but nevertheless important features of the external structure of *The Farmer's Boy* should be noted, for they begin a series of determinations with ramifications for the entire work. In his choices of subject and hence structure, Bloomfield moved from the eternal openness of invention to a series of closures by which he limited himself and the poem. His first wise choice was to write of what he knew and this, in Bloomfield's case, seems a considerable limitation. He chose too, to write of a subject that stirred his quieter passions. With each choice, he freed his genius to know his subject with a thoroughness and intensity which are commendable and perhaps unique. Each closure, too, gave Bloomfield the freedom to manage his subject in ways that would otherwise be impossible. The most obvious element of structure is the division of the poem into four books each dealing with a season passing on a Suffolk farm and each following the simple activities of Giles, the farmer's boy. Of the books "Spring", with which the poem begins, and "Autumn" are slightly shorter than the other two. Organic and changing as the seasons are, their very continuum establishes a structural and later a thematic unity for the poem. While Bloomfield knew Thomson, Goldsmith, and others, his structure seems to come directly from nature. Initially, this seasonal structure itself imposes a number of limitations on the artist and the work.

The great length of the poem and the temperate climate of Suffolk both conspire to limit the poet to descriptions of gradual change within a range of moderation. That removes the possibility of entertaining an audience with the extreme and capricious weather of other climates. Excluded are the alpine storms, desert winds, and rain forests which might have provoked tension, suspense, and the sublime or titillated his audience with expectations of the unusual. Since Bloomfield, Giles, and the audience all know that winter would come surely, gradually, all would be looking elsewhere for the wholly unknown or unexpected, if indeed it would be anticipated at all.

Having given the structure of the poem over to the natural cycle of the seasons, the artist finds some new things possible. Bloomfield is free to use the slight tension which arises from our expectations of the inevitable coming of a season or an expected event. With

predictable patterns established, any small variation within the
natural order can evoke pleasant reactions in his audience.
Bloomfield argues, for example, against the usual expectations
surrounding the hard season of winter by treating it as a welcomed
time of rest and delights. And spring with its stereotypes of blooms,
rejuvenation, and gamboling lambs he sets against the realities of
death and butchering which make the transition to summer a
welcomed change.

The seasonal continuum allows Bloomfield to display the same
scenes in contrasting seasons; full descriptions of the minute scenes
and events of rural life won him his strongest praise. From those
scenes comes a quiet sense of the continuity of rural life so interre-
lated with the seasons.

Another of the choices or closures which Bloomfield makes is that
of a particularized, local setting that he knew intimately and loved
well. The setting becomes both servant and determiner of structure.
What Bloomfield chooses, of course, is his uncle's farm where he
had lived as "the farmer's boy." As I indicated in chapter 1, Mr.
Austin's farm was in Sapiston, not far from Bloomfield's boyhood
home, and, significantly enough, it was a part of the manor of the
duke of Grafton. Although the duke did become Bloomfield's most
faithful patron, it is more important to the structure and meaning of
the poem that Mr. Austin was a tenant farmer in the open-field
system of agriculture. That system, which enclosure and other
forces had largely destroyed by the time of the poem's composition,
was viewed by Bloomfield, as well as by other champions of rural
life, as the basis of those social and ethical values he most admired.

That the setting is both servant and determiner of the greater
structure may be seen in the ways it both unifies and limits the
poem. There is, in fact, a sense in which the use of a single locale,
with a single central character *is* the unity of the poem, although the
seasons, the tone, the style, and a host of other factors contribute to
it. In this sense, *The Farmer's Boy* is about the meaning of a small
farm in Suffolk and a small boy's experience of that place. These
limitations seem to be coordinate with those imposed by selecting a
seasonal arrangement in a temperate climate.

The closure that Bloomfield experienced in selecting Mr. Austin's
farm produces other, specific limitations. What the poet has to
describe, to make images from, is the small farm itself and the
experience, things, and life he had known there. Certainly, that is

not all there was to life or the world, yet any statement the poet
wishes to make or any vision he wishes to present was bound,
following his choice, to come from there. Although Thomson had
been Bloomfield's first model, he specifically disclaims Thomson's
range or any range too far beyond the simple English farm:

> No deeds of arms my humble lines rehearse,
> No *Alpine* wonders thunder through my verse,
> The roaring cataract, the snow-topt hill,
> Inspiring awe, till breath itself stands still:
> Nature's sublimer scenes ne'er charm'd mine eyes,
> Nor Science led me through the boundless skies;
> From meaner objects far my raptures flow:
> O point these raptures! bid my bosom glow![10]

Again, Bloomfield both recognizes and sacrifices certain standard
devices with which he might have moved and excited his audience.
The sacrifice here is one of spectacular material which he exchanges
for a common subject with which a great part of his audience would
be at least marginally acquainted. If his book was to be read by his
mother, who knew the setting, and by other Englishmen who had
been led to the city by forces not unlike those which led the poet,
then Bloomfield assumes the great burden of accuracy and authenticity. Proof that such a burden existed was published in 1806, when
Joseph Holland, disturbed to find no mention of haying in
Bloomfield's poem, produced *An Appendix to the Season of Spring,
in the Rural Poem, The Farmer's Boy*, "to right the matter."[11]
Bloomfield, if he were greatly concerned with verisimilitude, would
also be constrained from taking flights of fancy incompatible with his
realism.

A single, particularized setting also provides the poet with a
number of freedoms. The restricted setting opens the possibility of
an extensive and detailed examination of its contents. The "meaner
objects" which Bloomfield claims for his study assume a far greater
significance than if dwarfed by mountains or vast plains. With those
objects unchallenged, he can prove them fit for poetry, elevate their
importance, and as he changes their seasonal garb, create in them a
fullness and complexity.

If the audience's familiarity with his subject compels him to great
accuracy, it also frees him to excite its sense of recognition by
presenting familiar objects, traditions, concerns, and themes. To

those in his audience come recently to the smoky streets and crowded quarters of the city, the recognition of their own past rural life could evoke at once a painful nostalgia and a comforting awareness that their past was still real. Few of his city-bred readers would have been so divorced from rural life that they had not seen glimpses of it during country walks or heard it spoken of by others newly come to the city, or read of it in children's tales, magazines, or that descriptive type of travel literature which dealt with their own country.

The poet is also free to discover and examine what universal experience he might extract from his particular setting. In selecting carefully which of young Giles's experiences he will portray, Bloomfield can display those experiences that he feels *should* be universal—those rural lessons of which the city dweller is forever deprived. And if it follows that the human mind can idealize best when it has experienced what is real, Bloomfield's restricting choice opens to him the possibility of idealizing or even mythologizing his setting. More than by simple selectivity, he idealizes and gives meaning to his setting by a careful arrangement of its contents. In "Summer" he can move from a humorous and specific picture of a self-important gander which stalks the barnyard, to a more awesome but nonetheless specific picture of a summer storm, and finally to the emotional fullness and comfort of the feast of harvest-home. The structure of his emotional argument, by which he makes winter a welcomed event, heightens and idealizes the reader's perception of the setting in the same manner. The tranquility of setting seen in the sheepfold in "Winter" is accented, set off to best advantage, by appending it to a scene in which Giles mistakes a familiar ash tree for some spectral figure and is terrified by it.

Bloomfield's structuring of the poem is also the structuring of an argument, an emotional one. Certainly such an argument would be enhanced and strengthened if it matched the natural passions, predilections, and loves of the speaker, if it spoke directly of his personal concerns. Mr. Austin's farm, then, is the ideal setting for Bloomfield's statement, for it was the place of his first loves and was itself a first love. The common ground of the country experience on which both author and readers can stand is, no matter what dissimilar paths lead them there, a valuable place where Bloomfield can both gain his reader's trust and lead them to heightened passions for the rural land. Once sharing Bloomfield's knowledge and eventually his fondness for the rural way of life, the audience would find doubly effective his authorial intrusions showing the encroachments of urban life on the country or those comparing the more ideal life to that of the city.

The intrusions too, become structural devices which break the flow of rural description and narration much as the city intrudes into the regularity of rural life, and their very nature, disruptive and digressive, demands that the reader attend to a salient point of the emotional argument. Thus in "Spring," when the poet celebrates Suffolk cheese as an item of past regional pride, he stops to speak of the city and its demands which have ruined the quality of the cheese. The fondness of the audience for rural scenes, again, did free Bloomfield to please with the familiar; he could touch on scenes of the ideal or half-remembered ways of life, or he could shape the limitations of setting, accepted by both him and his readers, into the most forceful argument possible. Such patterned emotional argument had been structured by Goldsmith years earlier in *The Deserted Village*, but Bloomfield's approach to the matter is significantly different.

There is a final way in which Bloomfield imposed limitations on the structure of *The Farmer's Boy*. The central figure in the poem, Giles the farmer's boy, is a gentle, inquisitive, sometimes stumbling eleven- or twelve-year-old. That Bloomfield chooses to circumscribe much of the experience of the poem within the reach of such a lad may indicate that he wished to recapture as accurately as possible his own rural experience. Giles becomes a sympathetic character who not only limits the poem but also contributes to its structural unity. He is not presented as a strictly autobiographical creature. In speaking of him, Bloomfield retires to the relative objectivity of third person and treats his adventures with humor as well as sympathy.

Giles's very presence in all of the books, however, does bind the poem together. When Bloomfield asks his audience to view rural England over Giles's shoulder, so to speak, the omniscient point of view is considerably telescoped and limited. Any mechanical application of this device which would have the reader following every wag of the boy's head would be, of course, most disconcerting, and the poet avoids this danger without letting the poem slip too far beyond what Giles did see or hear or learn. A picture of a rural maid in the harvest field, for example, is all but completed before we realize that Giles is even present. The reader feels that he is experiencing the events with Giles rather than through him; the constancy of this device itself is another contribution to unity. It is distinctly old-fashioned, in a sense, that Bloomfield should not allow himself, his own emotional experience and the nature of his perceptions, to be central to his poems. The subject, instead, is nature itself, rural life itself.

With such a character as Giles, the poet can present rural life with some of the same order, limitation, freshness, and artless simplicity of reaction that he himself had at Giles's age. That certainly would not be art of itself, but the poet who speaks of Giles might order the boy's experience into an aesthetically pleasing whole. The poet can, if he wishes, fashion Giles's experience as support for his argument. With a crude emotional validity and energy the truths of a rural boyhood flow from Bloomfield's past into his picture of Giles and the country, now ordered, structured, arranged with an emotion of the present tense. Significantly, Bloomfield writes almost the whole of the poem in present tense, not differentiating between invocations to his muse, addresses to the seasons, the story of Giles, or the description of rural scenes. Emotional energies from past experience and present feelings for the country are in this way bound together. Here may be one more explanation of why his readers came to think of him as the farmer's boy.[12]

Having examined the skeletal outlines of the structure of *The Farmer's Boy* and several of the factors affecting it, let me suggest first that it is a structure designed to display most advantageously something that Bloomfield cherished. The general subject is rural life, and if he thought that valuable, there are a number of possible modes in which he might have presented his subject to his audience. He might, for example, have created a sweet, truly descriptive poem, lyrical in tone, and calculated to evoke appreciative sighs. There is no doubt that certain readers who closed their eyes to all but the lambs at play did just that. The complexity of the structure, which included death, blood, real labor and real sweat, however, denies that possible intent and, for any careful reader, that possible reaction.

Again, if he found rural life valuable, Bloomfield might have celebrated it with an ode, had he the training to write one or the kind of intellect that could have sustained one. The tone, however, is more the concern here than the form, and celebration is at the center of things. His invocation promises raptures flowing from mean objects, and he requests of his muse:

> O point these raptures! bid my bosom glow!
> And lead my soul to ecstasies of praise
> For all the blessings of my infant days!

(4)

His passionate description of the mean objects, all part of the "Blessings" of his infant days, done with the immediacy of present tense and set in a durable structure, holds rural life up for public acclaim and celebrates its beauties and mysteries. Celebration, then, might be the goal—purely and simply a mode of address designed to extol. But there are several considerations which dissuade me from such a view of Bloomfield's work and artistic intent.

There are within the structure of the poem a number of intrusions (comparing, asserting, and lamenting) in which the poet speaks forcefully of change and of the city and its effects on rural life. The first, in spring, which begins with as simple an occurrence as the changing quality of cheese and proceeds to indict the "Dependant [sic], huge Metropolis," has already been cited. Another is strategically located at the end of "Summer" where the reader has just experienced the joys of the harvest-home celebation. Giles disappears as our focus and as a character and a "mourner" who is presumably one of the older peasant-laborers recites what Bloomfield's "Argument" titles "Reflection, &c." It is a formal lament for the passing of the old rural order. Finally, a comparison of the lot of Dobbin, a plow horse, with that of a post-horse again indicts the urban ethic (or lack of one) which ignores the interdependency of man and nature. The address to Dobbin follows a demonstration of "Tenderness to Cattle" performed by Giles and a section of moral instruction in which the farmer lectures Giles on the humanitarian significance of his humble duties. Here again the placement or arrangement of the intruding comparison is important.

If these and several similar devices were less clearly connected to the movement of the whole poem, they might be considered nothing more than intrusions. The poem might be a simple lay celebrious of rural life written by a country-bred man whose urban experience prompts him to break in with a few inevitable comparisons intended to assure his audience of his preference for the country and designed (if indeed they had a design) to intensify and complement his description of the farm. I have suggested, however, that Bloomfield's management of the structure of the poem creates what might be called an emotional argument, that he so arranges the description and episodes as to persuade his readers of the importance of certain scenes, episodes, and statements. Hence, the progress of the narrative and description which leads to the harvest-home scene in "Summer" focuses the reader's awareness on that scene. We come to it with our emotions heightened, persuaded of the scene's importance. What follows immediately is the "mourner's" lamentation of change, and it is there that Bloomfield makes his point. It appears that the intrusions are digressive in nature, digressive, I think, in the sense that they are discursive statements tangentially supporting a larger argument contained in the rest of the poem.

With the clue taken from these digressions, I suggest that the mode of Bloomfield's address was indeed celebration, but he chose that style within a context of argumentation. That he celebrates to persuade his audience, that he celebrates at times in an elegiac tone, and that he does in fact, essay a consciously persuasive discourse will be demonstrated in the course of a close look at the style and thematic content of the poem.

III *Spring: Invoking the Muse and Limiting the Scope*

Bloomfield calls his work *The Farmer's Boy; A Rural Poem*, and whether he thought it a pastoral poem or a peasant poem or a rural poem is best left for a later discussion. For the present it may be helpful to observe his other choices of titles. *Rural Tales, Ballads, and Songs* again chooses the term "rural," while *Wild Flowers; or, Pastoral and Local Poetry* balances the perhaps more elevated term "pastoral" with the specific indication that this is "local" or rural English poetry. Even "Hazelwood Hall," which he refers to in his letters as a "pastoral drama,"[13] he prints as "A Village Drama." Whatever else might be concluded from his titles, I will assume that he wishes his audience to give primacy to the fact that his is poetry about things rural, more specifically English rural things, and not to what he does with or in the pastoral tradition.

His argument for the book of "Spring" gives no real clue to persuasive or didactic intent; it speaks only of his invocation and of

rural occupations, events, and things. His invocation begins in what
Edmund Blunden called "Thomsonian tone, Goldsmithian measure," hence "in feeling genuine, in utterance borrowed."[14] But
hear Bloomfield:

> O come, blest Spirit, whatsoe'er thou art,
> Thou rushing warmth that hovers round my heart,
> Sweet inmate, Hail, thou source of sterling joy,
> That poverty itself cannot destroy,
> Be thou my Muse; and faithful still to me,
> Retrace the paths of wild obscurity.
>
> (3)

The elevated tone, of course, is not Bloomfield's best. He manages
some effects, however, that deserve consideration. There is some
mystery and even a touch of humor in the invocation to a spirit the
writer himself cannot identify, but the humor vanishes in the little
thicket of ambiguities he creates.

Unlike Thomson, his chief literary source, Bloomfield does not
directly address Spring, although she may be in his mind. The spirit
is identified as an inmate of his heart, his present emotions, and
whether she is Spring or a bit less probably, a rural sprite who lives
there through memory we are not told. Too, she could be both—a
vernal spirit inhabiting the English countryside, recalled from his
youth to present life. All of these possibilities could be sources of joy
capable of withstanding the press of poverty, for Bloomfield's urban
years before and during the composition of the poem were leaner
still than his boyhood.

Most probably the spirit he addresses is connected to the emotional force of his rural past remembered and made real in a new
sense. It is as if without benefit of Wordsworth's "Preface" he
invoked "those thoughts and feelings which, by his [the poet's] own
choice, or from the structure of his own mind, arise in him without
immediate external excitement."[15] She is indeed related to memory
or recollection, but she is not memory for her task is to "Bear me
through regions where gay Fancy dwells;/But mount to Truth's fair
form what Memory tells" (4).

I excluded the possibility of this invocation being addressed to the
season, as Thomson's are, with these considerations. Unlike Thomson's direct address, "Come, gentle Spring, ethereal mildness,
come,"[16] Bloomfield, who can be most specific, is not. Unlike *The*

Seasons, The Farmer's Boy was first conceived as a piece, as a whole cyclic work, so that Bloomfield would more naturally design an invocation for the entire poem and hence for all the seasons. Bloomfield's lines, however, may serve as a beckoning to spring.

To return to the edge of the small verbal thicket, there are finally those "paths of wild obscurity" to consider. Their "wildness" hints that the poet will not present the same structured vision of nature Thomson had offered in his description of the season "as it affects the various parts of nature, ascending from the lower to the higher."[17] By "obscurity" Bloomfield no doubt meant "remoteness," but there is in the term the conscious suggestion of the humility and inconspicuousness of his subject.

There follow those previously examined lines in which Bloomfield at once rejects some subjects and defines his own territory. Naturally, his muse would not be Calliope; thankfully, it will not be the spirit of Thomson. A gesture in recognition of his own limitations follows: "Nature's sublimer scenes ne'er charm'd mine eyes,/Nor Science led me through the boundless skies" (4). Such a disclaimer may reveal a distinctive feature of the speaker whose ethic demands a poetry of real experience. Such poetry, the voice asserts, could have its ecstasy even from the "meaner objects" of Nature and would have it from the known, from the experienced, presented with whatever verisimilitude possible. When in the next lines he turns to the things and events of humble rural life, he addresses them with such joy and simple dignity that the reader can forget their lack of elevation. Here Bloomfield, like Crabbe in *The Village,* has as part of his subject rural life in the vanishing open-fields system of agriculture, but he does not borrow Crabbe's emphasis on "the real Picture of the Poor." Instead Bloomfield balances the "joys and cares" of rural life and sees what sorrows he finds there as "quick springing" and "transient as the dew" (4).

As Giles is introduced, Bloomfield's style becomes in Edmund Blunden's words "better and more homely." Such stylistic improvement can be seen elsewhere in the poem, too, when Bloomfield moves from a more general statement in which the emphasis is on his speaker's public voice to a scene involving Giles or a rural picture where speaker and voice more nearly blend with the subject:

> 'Twas thus with *Giles:* meek, fatherless, and poor;
> Labour his portion, but he felt no more;

> No stripes, no tyranny his steps pursu'd;
> His life was constant, cheerful, [*sic*] servitude. . . .
>
> (5)

With the introduction of the theme of benevolence, here the benevolence of Giles's employer, the contrast with Crabbe's picture becomes even more apparent. Bloomfield does not deny the life of labor or the poverty but introduces other characteristics which balance the tone of the portrayal. Through Giles ("The fields his study, Nature was his book," 5) the reader's expectations of pictures of the revolving seasons are established and the constancy of good amidst the pleasant and unpleasant reality is argued: "Though every change still varied his employ, / Yet each new duty brought its share of joy" (5).

The structure next echoes Thomson's dedication to the countess of Hartford; the description, however, is more specific:

> Where noble Grafton spreads his rich domains,
> Round *Euston's* water'd vale, and sloping plains,
> Where woods and groves in solemn grandeur rise,
> Where the kite brooding unmolested flies;
> The woodcock and the painted pheasant race,
> And sculking foxes, destin'd for the chace. . . .
>
> (5)

It is important, I think, that this region, its creatures and its rhythms were all comprehensible to a simple country lad. One of the first differences between rural and urban life may lie there in what is knowable and what is known. Giles knew and was taught by Nature (6), and he knew his employer as a man of great hospitality, who was "Serv'd from affection, for his worth rever'd" (6). When the farmer with his eye for "unceasing industry" finds a constant supply of jobs for the boy, he may be serving as a teacher of the knowable from which a man may draw identity, a function the later books picture more clearly.

That Bloomfield knew Thomson but used his model with economy and a true sense of his own purpose can be observed in their treatments of departing winter. Thomson in language characteristically more elevated and less specific describes Nature at her extremes:

> And see where surly Winter passes off
> Far to the north, and calls his ruffian blasts;
> His blasts obey, and quit the howling hill,
> The shattered forest, and the ravaged vale;
> While softer gales succeed, at whose kind touch,
> Dissolving snows in livid torrents lost,
> The mountains lift their green heads to the sky.[18]

Bloomfield, whose concern was with the delicate effects of spring on the Suffolk countryside, says simply: *"Fled* now the sullen murmurs of the North, / The splendid raiment of the *Spring* peeps forth" (6). Finding his own ground, Bloomfield proceeds with his delightfully sure, clear description of the countryside and of the seasonal activities.

Plowing, he argues, is properly the business of a plowman and his well-trained team of horses; "No groaning ox is doom'd to labour there" (7). The use of plowboys or a goad to move the animals along is unnecessary, for it seems in the natural order of things that the smiling plowman and his horse work in harmony as if both understand the full course of the toil and the nature of the enterprise. Giles follows the plowman first with a team and harrow, then again scattering grain, and finally over the same ground to bury the grain. Having invested considerable labor, Giles is well prepared to learn an obvious but important lesson about the limitations of human enterprise. Should a crop appear, it will be through the grace of Nature and God.

With the spring planting complete and the morrow in God's hands, the farmer turns a speculative eye to the future:

> In fancy sees his trembling oats uprun,
> His tufted barley yellow with the sun;
> Sees clouds propitious shed their timely store,
> And all his harvest gather'd round his door.
>
> (9)

Having such a vision while his crops are still in their infancy may be a natural thing for any farmer, but it is more, I think, than mere wishing and perhaps more than an exercise in faith. His vision is of a life that is largely knowable, a rare thing indeed. What urban man can look at his life and enterprise with a quiet sense of where he has been, where he is, and where he will go? Standing in his sprouting fields in the present, the farmer dreams of the future. His knowledge of the fruition of his enterprise is based upon the past, on other years of harvest, other seasons of toil. The plows, for example, are called "slumbering plows," and if they slumber, they must once have been at labor and will labor again. This is no land of Cockayne; until the labors of the next seasons are complete, the harvest is still a thing of fancy. Bloomfield, his farmer, and the reader, however, have now a set of reasonable expectations for the future.

The farmer's brief reverie also anticipates the structure of the next books of the poem. The reader knows where the poem is going, just as the farmer knows the course of his life in the next months. If the reader would forget the realities of effort and anxiety that remain before the harvest, Bloomfield provides them immediately, as it becomes Giles's duty to protect the fields from marauding birds. This structured, knowable existence, then, is one of the valuable parts of rural life which Bloomfield will defend. And having presented the theme, the poet will return to it variously in the rest of the poem.

Returning to Giles protecting the newly planted fields from the rooks which might destroy the new crop, we find yet another lesson. This episode describing the destructive birds is followed by an almost equal number of lines on the loveliness of songbirds. The resulting structural balance argues the importance of the balanced nature of rural life. The rooks and crows are indeed "formidable foes" (9). Capable of destroying the crop, they are clever enough to post a watch against any "sculking gunner"[19] and to recover swiftly from any terror the shots instill. They comprehend the true nature of a scarecrow, "harmless rifleman of rags and straw" (9), and are not kept away long by that perhaps more humane device. Such an enemy might prompt an argument for its destruction, and indeed Lofft must have feared that to be the case, for he appended to the text a long note on the value of rooks and crows as insect eaters. Bloomfield's advice, of course, is not the wholesale destruction of the pests.

Since they will not "heed such centinels [sic] that never move" (9), he advises the farmers to take a few slain birds, and:

> Let then your birds lie prostrate on the earth,
> In dying posture, and with wings strech'd forth;

Shift them at eve or morn from place to place,
And death shall terrify the pilfering race.

(10)

Delightfully human as Giles is, "never fam'd was he nor foremost found / To break the seal of sleep" (10), he is called from his bed to this grisly work by a morning scene that supplies the balance alluded to earlier. "All is delicacy, variety, regeneration,"[20] Blunden writes; the scene deserves lingering attention because in it again Giles is learning, the poet finding inspiration, the reader being persuaded:

> But when at day-break summon'd from his bed,
> Light as the lark that carol'd o'er his head.
> His sandy way deep-worn by hasty showers,
> O'er-arch'd with oaks that form'd fantastic bow'rs,
> Waving aloft their tow'ring branches proud,
> In borrow'd tinges from the eastern cloud,
> (Whence inspiration, pure as ever flow'd,
> And genuine transport in his bosom glow'd)
> His own shrill matin join'd the various notes
> Of Nature's music, from a thousand throats:
> The blackbird strove with emulation sweet,
> And Echo answer'd from her close retreat;
> The sporting white-throat on some twig's end borne,
> Pour'd hymns to freedom and the rising morn;
> Stopt in her song perchance the starting thrush
> Shook a white shower from the black-thorn bush,
> Where dew-drops thick as early blossoms hung,
> And trembled as the minstrel sweetly sung.

(10–11)

Twenty lines of clear, loving description do not in themselves make an argument, but for the present, it remains Bloomfield's purpose to show the reader that this is indeed a lovely scene full of a worthy kind of life. The cloistered, bowerlike scene Bloomfield arranges so that it opens onto a wide heath, sparkling with morning dews that reflect the sun's first rays toward the viewer. Although natural and real, the shift between these scenes is structured so as to move from an area necessitating close careful description to a wide and pleasing prospect. This is, of course, a technique well known to

eighteenth-century literary pictorialists. There on the heath Giles
comes to his first task, removing the dead rooks from the trees
where they hung safe from foxes and scattering them about the field
to ward off the living birds.

Giles returns to the barnyard where over the noise of the animals
and the dairymaid's clattering he is barely able to hear her cry, "*Go
fetch the cows . . .*" (12). The reader is reminded by the poet that
here is a far different chorus of noises from the one Giles had just
left. Still, the barnyard is far from an unpleasant place; it simply
lacks the loveliness of remoter nature. It is, instead, a source of sure
humor. When "pigs, and ducks, and turkies, throng the door, / And
sitting hens, for constant war prepared" (12), the germ of laughter is
already present. Bloomfield will not make fun of silly, crude rustics
and their surroundings. Bloomfield's phrasis in "And sitting hens,
for constant war prepared" is not an attempt to evoke the derisive
laughter of the burlesque—as any rural lad who has ever disturbed a
setting hen will testify. There is a very real fury in such a bird, and
the poet's figure is simply meant to express the incongruity.

Giles's next small labor is the summoning of the cows from
pasture to barnyard for the milking, and at his halloo they come in
their established order, reluctantly, sedately, with one "[a]llow'd
precedence, undisputed sway" (13). The cow yard that awaits them
has been cleaned:

> Thence from its chalky bed behold convey'd
> The rich manure that drenching winter made,
> Which pil'd near home, grows green with many a weed,
> A promis'd nutriment for Autumn's seed.

> (13–14)

Any poet who is capable of writing appreciatively about the *quality*
of manure cannot be all bad. Others, in fact some of note, have tried
such an appreciation. But Cowper's phrase, "stercoraceous heap," is
awkward and flat beside Bloomfield's. On this farm husbandry
proceeds with a fine sense of stewardship. The land is not raped for
what it will produce but is cultivated and improved naturally,
preserving the cycle of life, the balance between man and his
environs. Husbandry practiced by men who take their whole life
from the same soil that they devote their lives to is another of the
things of worth for which Bloomfield argues. This is husbandry as
proud of its cultivation, of its caretaking, as of its product.

The mistress of the farm, the milkmaid, and Giles are all involved
in the milking:

> And crouching *Giles* beaneath a neighbouring tree
> Tugs o'er his pail, and chants with equal glee;
> Whose hat with tatter'd brim, of knap so bare,
> From the cow's side purloins a coat of hair,
> Mottled ensign of his harmless trade,
> An unambitious, peaceable cockade.
>
> (14)

The unassuming fashion in which the mistress gives "cheerful aid"
in the joint effort may foreshadow yet another of Bloomfield's
themes—the properly fond relationship between the farmer and his
workers. The great detail with which the poet examines the rite of
milking supports the thought that man should have pride in the
rural arts themselves, as much as in their products. Giles himself
serves whatever natural need arises about him:

> A *Gibeonite*, that serves them all by turns:
> He drains the pump, from him the faggot burns;
> From him the noisy hogs demand their food;
> While at his heels run many a chirping brood,
> Or down his path in expectation stand,
> With equal claims upon his strewing hand.
>
> (15–16)

"How gentle and how powerful is this kind of harmony with
Nature," Edmund Blunden writes of the scene. "As one reads, one
almost demands nothing more complete and enigmatic."[21] The
mystery, as Bloomfield paints it, is in the way of living.

One product of the milking is the unrivaled Suffolk cheese, and
when produce finally emerges from the rural art Bloomfield digresses. The unrivaled cheese of the country is now "the well-known
butt of many a flinty joke" (16), for the heavy demands of the city on
this rural industry have perverted the cheese-making process.
Bloomfield's response is the following antiurban digression denig-
rating, first in general terms, the city:

> Provisions grave, thou ever craving mart,
> Dependant [*sic*], huge Metropolis! where Art
> Her poring thousands stows in breathless rooms,
> Midst pois'nous smokes and steams, and rattling looms;

> Where grandeur revels in unbounded stores;
> Restraint, a slighted stranger at their doors!
>
> (16)

The city by its very shape and needs denies harmony with nature. The balanced ethic of responsible husbandry has no place in the city which consumes and only consumes.

Bloomfield first condemns the city for its effects on the rural economy at large:

> Thou, like a whirlpool, drain'st the countries round,
> Till, London market, London price, resound
> Through every town, round every passing load,
> And dairy produce throngs the eastern road:
> Delicious veal, and butter, every hour,
> From Essex lowlands, and the banks of Stour;
> And further far, where numerous herds repose,
> From Orwell's brink, from Weveny, or Ouse.
>
> (17)

Then more specifically the urban demands on Suffolk are exposed:

> Hence Suffolk dairy-wives run mad for cream,
> And leave their milk with nothing but its name;
> Its name derision and reproach pursue,
> And strangers tell of "three times skimm'd sky-blue."

And the cheese, once made, is harder than a post, too hard to cut. Its destiny is often the hog-trough where it "rests in perfect spite, / Too big to swallow, and too hard to bite" (18). With more seriousness his apostrophe to the rural lands stands as a challenge to his countrymen to resist urban pressure that would corrupt careful husbandry:

> Inglorious victory! Ye Cheshire meads,
> Or Severn's flow'ry dales, where plenty treads,
> Was your rich milk to suffer wrongs like these,
> Farewell your pride! farewell renowned cheese!
> The skimmer dread, whose ravages alone
> Thus turn the mead's sweet nectar into stone.
>
> (18)

Rayner Unwin is correct in asserting that Bloomfield's didactic discourses are not done in the manner of a farmer's boy.[22] He speaks as poet and as rural man. When his beliefs about rural life are threatened by the intrusions of urbanization, he protests, sometimes emotionally, and condemns those negative forces by contrast with what could and should be. True to this pattern of argument, he follows the Suffolk-cheese digression with more vernal scenes in which his technique is once more loving, careful, and precise.

The most frequently anthologized of these scenes is the "Lambs at Play" section where Giles is present again and the poet's soul is able to pursue its "darling theme" (19). The sheep are kept safely in fields where the "heath's rough produce" will not mar their fleece. Still, they are free to seek within that limitation the "Enchanting spirit, dear variety" (19)—a pattern not unlike that of rural life itself. The scene around the lambs is a fairy-piece, and Bloomfield pauses in it to address his readers. Did those who knew the spring, who had felt and seen it not give way to the "thrilling transport?" The questions give way to an invitation to the experience and emotion. Those readers who lack their own rural experience are given an invitation that enumerates some of what they could gain by sharing:

> Ye who can smile, to wisdom no disgrace,
> At the arch meaning of a kitten's face;
> If spotless innocence, and infant mirth,
> Excites to praise, or gives reflection birth;
> In shades like these pursue your fav'rite joy,
> Midst Nature's revels, sports that never cloy.
>
> (21)

The lambs play until they cannot run, rest panting, and yet:

> A bird, a leaf, will set them off again:
> Or, if a gale with strength unusual blow,
> Scatt'ring the wild-briar roses into snow,
> Their little limbs increasing efforts try,
> Like the torn flower the fair assemblage fly.
>
> (22)

The loveliness of flying lambs and petals, however, is short lived. The fallen roses become for the lambs the "sad emblem of their doom" as the butcher comes to demand the firstlings of the flock. Although spared the sight, Giles learns the reality of death:

> His gay companions *Giles* beholds no more;
> Clos'd are their eyes, their fleeces drench'd in gore;
> Nor can Compassion, with her softest notes,
> Withhold the knife that plunges through their throats.
>
>   (22–23)

The mawkishness that might characterize the scene never appears. The closest Bloomfield comes to a sentimental ejaculation is in these lines: "Down, indignation! hence, ideas foul! / Away the shocking image from my soul!" (23). And with the real gore of butchery preceding it, this may well be justified. Too, Bloomfield reaches for a surprising effect with the gore. As I have suggested, the usually regenerative season of spring can be left now with relief, not longing. Pleasant and unpleasant experiences propel the reader through the seasons toward a reconciliation in the return to this scene at the close of the poem.

A final note is due the season. Rayner Unwin has proposed that this final scene is one of Bloomfield's arguments against something, specifically against the "murd'ring Butcher."[23] If this is true, it is the only time that Bloomfield argues against something without suggesting an alternate course, a better way, or a cure. The butchering, to be sure, is not a thing Bloomfield prizes or delights in, but it is a reality of rural life that he portrays unflinchingly as he might any other unpleasant necessity. This is "murder" in the sense of brutal slaughter, no more or no less brutal than the Old Testament sacrifice. And what rural life here consumes it will later replenish.

IV "*Summer*"

"Summer now enters, and, from a poetical point of view, not at all well," Edmund Blunden writes.[24] Bloomfield begins: "*The Farmer's* life displays in every part / A moral lesson to the sensual heart*" (37). Blunden is correct. The moral lesson that the speaker presents, however, does contain a further enunciation of the essence of the rural life that Bloomfield favors. Comparison with a similar didactic passage in "Winter" of Thomson's *Seasons* finds Thomson belaboring the lessons contained in all of nature and in the refined retirement to rural life, a vision far different from Bloomfield's. Bloomfield writes of his farmer:

> Though in the lap of plenty, thoughtful still,
> He looks beyond the present good or ill;

Nor estimates alone one blessing's worth,
From changeful seasons, or capricious earth;
But views the future with the present hours,
And looks for failures as he looks for show'rs.

(27)

The pattern of rural life in Suffolk in the eighteenth and nineteenth centuries—of moderate pace, reasonable surety, and acceptable limitations—appears to have promoted the natural order of things. The farmer, again, can stop at a given point in the orderly progression of his life and evaluate what is around him, discovering the cautions and promises of the future. His vision rests, as I have suggested, on the past. That his estimate of present plenty and future promise is circumspect may be natural for one directly dependent on the benevolence of nature. As the farmer weighs each blessing within the context of a larger, ordered, and knowable life structure, he shares something of Thomson's world view. Bloomfield's argument for rural life, however, differs from Thomson's as living a rural life differs from retiring to the country. If Bloomfield declines when his picture of the rural is searched for cosmic significances, his ascendancy comes when he is asked in human and natural terms the meaning of the rural life he knew in Suffolk.

Unlike those of technological man, the considered actions of the farmer flow from the lessons of the past. Moral deductions about them have the appearance of cliché, but those actions take place in a world at once more real and specific than Thomson's and more balanced with humor than Crabbe's. When the farmer "[f]or casual as for certain want prepares" (27) by sowing turnip seeds for winter fodder, the future inhabits the present, the structure of the poem is tightened, and the moral lesson to come in "Winter" is foreshadowed. It is, as Edmund Blunden suggests, "a task of faith."[25] If performing it furthers Giles's education, it also persuades the reader that there might be something here worth learning. The language is renewed and the cliché avoided.

When Giles once more has the task of harrowing, it is in dry soil that resists his labors, and Bloomfield offers an aphoristic bit of wisdom built by analogy on the rural experience:

E'en thus the living clod, the stubborn fool,
Resists the stormy lectures of the school,
Till tried with gentler means, the dunce to please,

His head imbides right reason by degrees;
As when from eve till morning's wakeful hour,
Light, constant rain, evinces secret pow'r,
And ere the day resume its wonted smiles,
Presents a cheerful easy task for *Giles*.

(29)

Although this is not Bloomfield's best writing, the enlightened patience that the poet suggests is a sure result of rural experience. The harrowing is quickly replaced with another task, that of keeping flocks of sparrows out of the ripening wheat, and the structure of the poem advances on the chronology of labor.

Giles has come to love his rural surroundings; he lingers in the border of the field where "*Wisdom's* placid eye delighted sees / His frequent intervals of lonely ease" (31). There, almost passively, Giles is touched by a wisdom that comes as slow revelation, a gradual learning through the senses and the emotions. Once stirred in this fashion he will always find delight in solitude. The result of the experience is that "heaven-directed thought his bosom warms" (31), thus establishing a pattern of knowledge vaguely akin to that described by the eighteenth-century philosopher David Hartley. Giles indulges in what Edmund Blunden calls "something like pecking with the sparrow, and more permissible."[26]

Just where the parting bough's light shadows play,
Scarce in the shade, nor in the scorching day,
Stretch'd on the turf he lies, a peopled bed,
Where swarming insects creep around his head.
The small dust-colour'd beetle climbs with pain
O'er the smooth plantain-leaf, a spacious plain!
Thence higher still, by countless steps convey'd
He gains the summit of a shiv'ring blade,
And flirts his filmy wings, and looks around,
Exulting in his distance from the ground.
The tender speckled moth here dancing seen,
The vaulting grasshopper of the glossy green,
And all prolific *Summer's* sporting train,
Their little lives by various pow'rs sustain.

(31–32)

Giles's contemplation of the tiny scene and Bloomfield's delicate precision in writing of it offer to the reader a momentary perception of the minute and intricate structure of life. Bloomfield's tone remains loving just as Giles's act of observation is loving. Both see; both are aware that here is something valuable; both strive to understand.

Understanding the mystery and meaning of what he sees, however, is beyond the present capability of Giles: "But what can unassisted vision do? / What, but recoil where most it would pursue" (32). This, of course, is a most unromantic view, and Bloomfield in questioning unassisted genius and natural sagacity shows a strong tie to the conservative writers of the eighteenth century. Still, Giles understands what is important if not the why of it. The skylark calls him on to new perceptions and new awareness, and he reluctantly quits his patient watching. The invitation to the reader ("You come too," Frost wrote) is clear but unspoken.

His hat rolled up for a telescope "to dull the glaring light," Giles watches the bird, then falls into the full and guilt-free sleep of one who has labored, found harmony with his world, and caught a moment of inner satisfaction. However rhapsodic even a prose account of the sleep of fulfillment may become, Bloomfield would have his readers believe it is a reality easily found in rural life. Again, the distinction between this experience and that open to the man who simply retires to the country is important, for Giles has his afternoon of contentment despite, even because of, the harsher realities of farm life with which he lives.

The joys of the skylark and of sleep are followed by description of the ripening crops, and over the plowman's shoulder the reader sees the fulfillment of his efforts in the golden fields. But it is the labor itself and the doing of it that must bring rural man his moment of pride, for rightfully as Bloomfield insists, from germination to maturity it was Nature's labor that produced the crop:

> . . . Heaven's munificence makes all the show,
> O'er every field and golden prospect found,
> That glads the ploughman's Sunday morning's round,
> When on some eminence he takes his stand,
> To judge the smiling produce of the land.
> Here Vanity slinks back, her head to hide:
> What is there here to flatter human pride?
>
> (33–34)

Then with a slightly antiurban touch, the effects of urban and rural wonders on man are explained:

> The tow'ring fabric, or the dome's loud roar,
> And stedfast columns, may astonish more,
> Where the charm'd gazer long delighted stays,
> Yet trac'd but to the *architect* the praise;
> Whilst here, the veriest clown that treads the sod,
> Without one scruple, gives the praise to *God*.
>
> (34)

The ripeness of the crops draws the rural folk to the field as if an emotional desire to be part of the harvest has lain dormant in them waiting the proper time. Again, the cyclic pattern of waking and sleeping things which have had past use and will be needed again is repeated in the sickle which nature calls "from its twelvemonth's rest" (34). The harvest is to benefit all:

> No rake takes here what Heaven to all bestows:
> Children of want, for you the bounty flows!
> And every cottage from the plenteous store
> Receives a burden nightly at its door.
>
> (35)

Such a cooperative, sharing ethic might seem vaguely subversive to the American city dweller with his beliefs in personal and private property. But to rural folk whose faith as well as practical observation tells them that the harvest comes from powers beyond their own, it is meet and right.

Harvest is a time of love and plenty. The farmer leaves the cool comfort of his house to enter the lively converse of the fields. There is even an echo of the pastoral singing match as "rival wits with more than rustic grace / Confess the presence of a pretty face" (36), and Bloomfield introduces another of the lovely things of rural life. The charming and humorous picture of the girl Mary who has joined the men in the harvest field is neither bawdy nor sexless:

> In youth's own bloom and native smiles array'd;
> Her hat awry, divested of her gown,
> Her creaking stays of leather, stout and brown; . . .
> Invidious barrier! why art thou so high,
> When the slight cov'ring of her neck slips by,
> There half revealing to the eager sight
> Her full, ripe bosom, exquisitely white?
> In many a local tale of harmless mirth,
> And many a jest of momentary birth,

> She bears a part, and as she stops to speak,
> Strokes back the ringlets from her glowing cheek.
>
> (36–37)

And as the hours decline and thirsts rise, Bloomfield again echoes the pastoral tradition while separating himself from its more refined manifestations. The bowl does not simply revert to the cup; it becomes even more rustic:

> Thirst rages strong, the fainting spirits fail,
> And ask the sov'reign cordial, home-brew'd ale:
> Beneath some shelt'ring heap of yellow corn
> Rests the hoop'd keg, and friendly cooling horn,
> That mocks alike the goblet's brittle frame,
> Its costlier potions, and its nobler name.
>
> (37)

Even Giles has a respite from his dusty task of carting the corn into the cobwebbed barn as he sips the brew.

The structure of Bloomfield's argument demands that having pleased his readers he instruct once more. The careless practice of docking horses' tails, like other ill-conceived notions that at times pass for agrarian reform and innovation, leave the animals in a miserable state:

> The bold assailants that surround thine head,
> Poor patient *Ball!* and with insulting wing
> Roar in thine ears, and dart the piercing sting:
> In thy behalf the crest-wav'd boughs avail
> More than thy short-clipt remnant of a tail,
> A moving mockery, a useless name,
> A living proof of cruelty and shame.
>
> (38–39)

A similar torture plagues newly shorn ewes, and the cows, best able to defend themselves against the insect swarm, kick over their pails. To balance this dark vision of man-made and natural plagues, the poet quickly introduces a comic tyrant, the gander, "spiteful, insolent, and bold" who threatens all the creatures of the barnyard until he encounters the "strolling swine":

> Happy the man that foils an envious elf,
> Using the darts of spleen to serve himself.

> As when by turns the strolling *Swine* engage
> The utmost efforts of the bully's rage,
> Whose nibbling warfare on the grunter's side
> Is welcome pleasure to his bristly hide;
> Gently he stoops, or lays himself along,
> Enjoys the insults of the gabbling throng.
>
> (40–41)

Bloomfield shifts his mood again with a description of twilight and the approaching summer storm. The real dangers of the storm and the farmer's relief at its passing lead at last to the feast of harvest-home. It is a celebration, Bloomfield argues, greater than the celebration of epic victory. Here at the climax of the second book, where the reader has possessed even more of the value and joy of rural life, Bloomfield again presses his argument. An important part of what he values in the harvest-home is the equal congress of all rural folk:

> Here once a year Distinction low'rs its crest,
> The master, servant, and the merry guest,
> Are equal all. . . .
>
> (45)

When the happy effect of this cordiality upon the plowman is shown, Bloomfield's readers are prepared with an awareness of its value. And they are prepared to accept the Goldsmithian somberness of the digression that follows the poet's sudden shift of tense:

> Such were the days, . . . of days long past I sing,
> When Pride gave place to mirth without a sting;
> Ere tyrant customs strength sufficient bore
> To violate the feelings of the poor;
> To leave them distanc'd in the mad'ning race:
> Where'er Refinement shews its hated face.
>
> (45–46)

The first indication that what he sings is past or passing is strategically placed halfway through the poem after the reader has been allowed to experience the valuable as what is, as what exists in the present world.

The new refinement, Bloomfield reasons, is the worst enemy of the peasant:

> '[T]is the peasant's curse,
> That hourly makes his wretched station worse;
> Destroys life's intercourse; the social plan
> That rank to rank cements, as man to man:
> Wealth flows around him, fashion lordly reigns;
> Yet poverty is his, and mental pains.
>
> (46)

Bloomfield argues here neither for economic reform nor for revolutionary social change, in the sense of new freedoms or new rights. Further, he does not wish to return to the world of the past; too much of the present and of the possible future excite him. He wishes, instead, to preserve what was good in rural life and to take it along into the future. Frequently the good he sees is in the human values of dignity, kindness, and social intercourse based upon reasonable sentiment. By reasonable sentiment I mean something close to the conservative eighteenth-century writer's notion that reason should somehow circumscribe the emotions. For Bloomfield, however, sentiment is made reasonable and appropriate when it flows from the natural and social limitations of rural life. That, of course, is endangered by this new and false refinement.

Refinement causes him to hear a disembodied rural voice which speaks an elegiac complaint against the social coldness and the new "grandeur" that accompanies it. If the change is the result of wealth, the voice reasons, then wealth is an enemy that denies the peasant his rights and dignity. *Emulation* is the term the voice attaches to the change, and it is in spirit contrary to all the rural values Bloomfield presents. The social pattern behind the term appears to be that of certain landowners imitating urban values, and adopting a new sensibility which matches their new wealth and which considers rural life loutish and its people inferior. To the rural speaker, the change and the wealth result from a new bigness in farms and landholdings, a bigness that threatens all hope of "humble industry":

> "Can my sons share from this paternal hand
> The profits with the labours of the land?
> No; tho' indulgent Heaven its blessing deigns,
> Where's the small farm to suit my scanty means?"
>
> (47)

The harvest-home feast does stave off present want, but the spirits of dignity and equality that made tenable the seasons of poverty are absent:

> "Our annual feast, when Earth her plenty yields,
> When crown'd with boughs the last load quits the fields,
> The aspect still of ancient joy puts on;
> The aspect only, with the substance gone:
> The self-same Horn is still at our command,
> But serves none now but the plebeian band. . . ."
>
> (47–48)

The farmer too is absent; victim of the new refinement, he entertains selected guests and ignores the laboring folk. The result of all this, Bloomfield argues, is that all parties suffer. The laborers have the insult of inferiority added to the injury of poverty; the farmer with his refined guests finds his pleasure limited to that of one rank of folk. " 'Selected guests selected phrases claim!,' " runs the scheme (49).

The book of "Summer" ends with the rural speaker recounting the mutual joy of shaking his master's hand and repeating a phrase which signals a part of the usable past. " 'Let labour have its due,' " the elegaic voice intones, " '. . . then peace is mine' " (49). What Bloomfield sees and decries in these lines is part of the gradual process of urbanization that has come variously to almost every culture. An evaluation of urban life is neither necessary nor immediately important to this study or to Bloomfield. It is important, however, that he saw the process as a threat to things he thought valuable. Although he usually does not argue for a specific new course of political or social action, he does oppose enclosure, one of the most damaging of the forces that changed rural life. Bloomfield in his private life even dreamed of his own gesture that would negate enclosure, but such is not the usual end of his persuasion. Bloomfield wishes, as I have said, to preserve the good and the usable in rural experience. He moves in two ways to accomplish this: he attempts to create in his readers an awareness, perhaps even an emotional state that might persuade them to preserve the rural values, and he himself commits an act of preservation in his art.

V   "Autumn"

The two remaining books of *The Farmer's Boy* enlarge the same arguments and enrich the same themes. The style is unhurried as

Bloomfield lingers on the details of the declining year. The falling away from the description of summer's riches to the quiet elegy at the end of the second book forms a fine emotional bridge or transition to "Autumn." The season itself is not drawn as sad, although Giles is unhappy for the first time since the close of "Spring." The excitement of the hunt and of the change in weather will balance the tone and hold off sadness.

First, Giles becomes a swineherd and takes the creatures to feed on fallen acorns put down by the autumn squalls. Feasting on such "Hot thirsty food" sends the swine to the edge of a marshy pool where the abrupt flight of a skittish duck causes great fear in the pigs:

> The herd decamp with more than swinish speed,
> And snorting dash through sedge, and rush, and reed:
> Through tangling thickets headlong on they go,
> Then stop, and listen for their fancied foe;
> The hindmost still the growing panic spreads,
> Repeated fright the first alarm succeeds,
> Till Folly's wages, wounds and thorns, they reap.
>
> (55)

The early dark overtakes the herd, and they huddle beneath boughs full of roosting pheasants. Giles's calls do not move them, for they will not return until the wood has been emptied of its store of acorns.

The knowable life within the natural order of seasonal change sets the course of the season's labor:

> Beyond bleak *Winter's* rage, beyond the *Spring*
> That rolling Earth's unvarying course will bring,
> Who tills the ground looks on with mental eye,
> And sees next *Summer's* sheaves and cloudless sky;
> And even now, whilst Nature's beauty dies,
> Deposits SEED, and bids new harvests rise.
>
> (56)

And prudent husbandry, based on the experience of the past, indicates that seed for fall planting should be treated to protect it against the dangers of grubs, cold, and lapse of time. Giles is now busy with plowing, harrowing, and manuring and has rest only on Sunday. With the cycle of labor and rest introduced, the transition to a description of the poor village church is smooth.

Despite the poverty of the scene and the presence of a moldering graveyard, Bloomfield's elegiac tone is balanced first by a bit of humor and later by the close picture of the vitality of the church-goers. The pastor's horse is the only one of God's creatures who does not share Sunday's "sweets of ease," and "true to time and pace, is doom'd to plod, /To bring the Pastor to the *House of God*" (57).

The words of single syllable seem to plod, and the rhyme has an almost burlesque quality as it leaps from the ridiculousness of "plod" to the sublimity of "God." The description of the church itself seems to decry rural poverty, but it comes in the same close, loving tone as much of the rest of the poem. It is as if the poet thinks that even here in the inequitable mendicancy of rural life, there is something of worth:

> Mean structure; where no bones of heroes lie!
> The rude inelegance of poverty
> Reigns here alone: else why that roof of straw?
> Those narrow windows with the frequent flaw?
> O'er whose low cells the dock and mallow spreads,
> And rampant nettles lift their spiry heads,
> Whlst from the hollows of the tower on high
> The grey-cap'd daws in saucy legions fly.
>
> (58)

The first lines here, more general and "elevated" than those that surround them, are much better than Bloomfield's usual attempts at elevation. They are better, I think, because they are preceded by the whimsically humorous irony of one pastor's horse and are followed quickly and organically by the precise description at which the poet excels. These eight lines which lead away in the direction of Gray's "Elegy Written in a Country Churchyard" are brought up quickly, almost roughly, by the next couplet: "Round these lone walls assembling neighbors meet, / And tread departed friends beneath their feet" (58). The sharply reversing levels of thought and emotion seem almost out of control until the next verses complete the scene and the reader experiences the full reality of a small churchyard where one has little choice but to stand on the graves.

The sharp juxtaposing of life and death continues to pattern encounters for the reader which begin to approximate the casual but sure awareness the country folk have of each. Amid the fresh graves of their acquaintances, the plowmen gather to talk of their continuing labors. The farmers' boys, competing, "jump from hollow-sounding grave to grave." The scene is completed with the introduction of pretty village maids who sometimes stroll to the church seeking flirtations and even love. Death and love, youth and energy, age and rest, labor and poverty, and freshness and decay whirl together to the surprise of no one who has experienced rural life. That the poet did not hesitate to give them all life in a single scene may indicate that he found in them no contradiction or unevenness, for they are, of course, all part of the natural order.

Bloomfield's extraordinary tactics of transition set him apart from Crabbe, Cowper, and the meditative poets of the period. When he is in his best rural voice and not straining to handle material beyond his ken, his sharp turns of material and tone lend constant variety to verse which might otherwise have tended toward flatness. The technique could subject the reader to considerable bouncing about and lead to inappropriate diction, but it does not. The whole sounds and feels organic and dynamic. In general, Bloomfield's excellence at transition results from the happy confluence of voice and subject alluded to above. The easy shifts from pathos or elevation to humor or careful description of meaner objects are complemented by the casual, unaffected directness of the country speaker. Something akin to decorum prevents the speaker from lingering in any highly emotional or elevated tone: it is a natural reserve, a politeness bordering on shyness that seems wholly fitting to the persona. The quick transitions, the sharpnesses, connect easily to the contrasts inherent in rural life. And the whole is saved from giddy disparateness by the organic nature of the rural life described and by the steady voice of the rural speaker whose standing place is within the setting and culture he describes.

From the country lasses Bloomfield digresses to the melancholy story of one of their number who grew quite mad and spent her days weeping in a nameless grief. The episode is based on a real incident remembered from the poet's youth, but it fails to become the pleasing verse Bloomfield manages elsewhere. The reader, like Giles, is invited to enlarge his power of sympathy and be educated by the pains of another of God's creatures. This use of the pathetic as an educating force that teaches about the social nature of all life is repeated over and over again in the poem. Giles is usually the student, but there is an implicit invitation to the reader to learn or remember the lesson. The episode begins well enough with an accurate description of the girl's dementia, but it ends with a disconcerting echo of Mackenzie's *The Man of Feeling* in which a sympathetic passerby sheds a predictable tear for her plight. Significantly, the final reasons for extending sympathy to the girl, Poll, are that she in the isolation of her madness will never know certain of the social joys:

> Joys which the gay companions of her prime
> Sip, as they drift along the stream of time;
> At eve to hear beside their tranquil home
> The lifted latch, that speaks the lover come:
> *That* love matur'd, next playful on the knee
> To press the velvet lip of infancy:
> To stay the tottering step, the features trace; . . .
> Inestimable sweets of social peace!
>
> (62–63)

The poet's personal prayer that he be allowed to keep that social peace himself follows. There may be some autobiographical significance in this concern with madness and the poet's prayer for sanity and peace, but that is overshadowed by the more general demonstration of the sad life outside the natural rural order.

As the autumn advances and nature become less hospitable, Giles is sent to guard the newly sown fields against woodland birds. Alone and cold, he straightaway sets about constructing a hut from turf and thatch. His game, an exercise in self-sufficiency for "the Crusoe of the lonely fields," involves starting a small fire and gathering sloes and rose hips to roast upon it. When he wishes to entertain his small friends, however, the pleasures of the hut are marred, for his guests fail to arrive. Giles's unhappiness, like most that Bloomfield pictures, is based on the disruption of the natural social order that underlies rural life. An important pattern is repeated as Giles's social expectations are dashed, and when his social surroundings become unbearable, even the fields become prisons. As with the laborer at the feast of harvest-home, unhappy despite the fullness of Nature's yearly gifts around him, so here the private congress of man and nature is insufficient as the cause of happiness. It is man communing with men on the common ground of nature that both Giles and the laborer seek and that will appear repeatedly in Bloomfield's writings as one of the most worthy parts of rural life.

In the hunting scenes that follow it may be the social pattern of the event that Bloomfield prizes most. He describes the hunt at length in a sprightly and vigorous manner. The qualities of faith, constancy, and zeal that he remembers in one of the hounds pleased other men, too, for when it died, above its grave in a stone wall in Euston Park was inscribed, *"Foxes, rejoice! here buried lies your foe."* The congress of the hunt (men, dogs, fox, and the forces of Nature) is not designed for the mere enjoyment of blood and death. In the poem the chase is never brought to the kill by Bloomfield, who hated such cruel sports as bull-baiting. The hunt is more a ritualized extension of the natural order in which foxes do eat fowl, and dogs do chase foxes, and man does set his dogs after the fox with at least the justification of protecting the lesser creatures. Bloomfield ends the section with a picture of the fowl safely housed at night.

That Bloomfield would not object to the possible cruelty of the foxhunt may be explained in yet another way. The sport, which literature and film prompt the modern reader to envision as the exclusive province of the landed gentry, was in reality a great leveler of classes. It was a sport in which a man of any station could ride with a duke, and to the humble villagers, it was a bit of bright excitement for a winter's day, an interest that transcended class and wealth.[27] Bloomfield probably saw it as another part of the best of rural life in which the common dignity of man and the common ground of nature were recognized.

The third book closes with the promise of winter and the rest it may provide from autumn's frantic labors. There is the ancient promise, too, of spring that awaits only the passing of the coldest season to bestow its cheer again.

VI *"Winter"*

The final book begins with yet another lesson in proper social intercourse, and again the lesson is presented for Giles and the reader at once. "Pity executes what Reason wills," as the farmer and Giles bring what comfort they can to the animals in the snow and ice. The opening lines are a vague and perhaps unfortunate attempt at elevation, for as Edmund Blunden suggests, "the humanitarian gospel according to our Suffolk labourer is best presented in picture and anecdote."[28] Happily, Bloomfield soon has Giles before us breaking the ice off the waiting turnips:

> No tender ewe can break her nightly fast,
> Nor heifer strong begin the cold repast

> Till *Giles* with pond'rous beetle foremost go,
> And scatt'ring splinters fly at every blow;
> When pressing round him, eager for the prize,
> From their mixt breath warm exhalations rise.
>
> (79)

As Giles, invisible beneath a huge forkful of hay, crosses the barnyard to fill the tall racks, the cattle and swine steal mouthfuls from his fork.

Giles completes his kind task and retires to the warmth of a Christmas evening fire to share the joys of conversation with the master of the farm and the laborers. Giles, who is often the target of the innocent humor, soon hears his master turn catechizer and must follow the mental progress of the questions about the farm to be sure that he has failed at no chore. All of the tasks relate to the comfort of the farm's creatures and all of them should, the farmer assures, teach a social lesson: " 'Thine heart should feel, what thou may'st hourly see, /*That duty's basis is humanity* ' " (83). The lesson, "mild, as the vernal show'r," has practical application when the plowman who has slumbered through this familiar speech invites Giles to walk with him and care for the horses.

The life of the farm horse, which has labored and now rests, reflects rural life at large. It is an almost perfect existence if we forget the tail docking in summer.

> Thus full replenish'd, perfect ease possest,
> From night to morn alternate food and rest,
> No rightful cheer withheld, no sleep debar'd [*sic*],
> Their each day's labour brings its sure reward.
>
> (85)

Then in a distinctly antiurban digression, Bloomfield chides old Dobbin for not better appreciating his lot by comparing his with the fate of a post-horse that serves urban man in thankless, joyless labor. The post-horse is driven and whipped, not urged or encouraged, and the sounds of his labor, like many sounds of labor in the industrial city, have a "tiresome sameness" that helps kill the spirit. Even here, where Bloomfield risks dreadful verse in pursuing his argument, he avoids the sentimental excesses of Richard Jago and others who attempted didactic verse about kindness to animals.

Later, when Giles's duties as shepherd call him again from the fire's warmth, the sight of the clouds prompt what Edmund Blunden calls a "universalizing fancy . . . which not the deepest mystic would be ashamed to share":[29]

> Spotless as snow, and countless as they're fair;
> Scatter'd immensely wide from east to west,
> The beauteous 'semblance of a *Flock* at rest.
> These, to the raptur'd mind, aloud proclaim
> Their MIGHTY SHEPHERD'S everlasting Name.
>
> (91–92)

Then humorously, fittingly, and naturally, young Giles whose imagination has been stirred has another vision. This time, however, he sees a "grisly *Spectre*" which frightens him half to death before he discovers that it is only a friendly ash tree dressed awesomely by the new season.

I have suggested in the initial discussion of the structure of the poem that Bloomfield inverts the reader's usual expectations for the seasons of spring and winter in his treatment of the subject of sheep and that he uses the sheep to achieve a structural unity. Lambs died a bloody death at the close of "Spring"; now the flock in the midst of "Winter" is all serenity and full, pregnant promise. Giles is there to protect them against any possible danger or want; and if a possible danger from the farmer's hungry mastiff seems a bit contrived, consider how much more satisfying this attempt at realism is than the pastorals of Ambrose Philips with their invented wolves. With the example of unexpected acts by hounds and even gentle pointers, acts that thwart "the gen'ral instinct of his race," we are better prepared to entertain possible violence by a mastiff.

All danger, however, is thwarted by the presence of Giles who counts his "heavy sided ewes" while "Surrounding stillness tranquilize his breast, / And shape the dreams that wait his hours of rest" (95). Giles is learning again from his rural surroundings. Following this peaceful image, winter begins to slip away from the fields, and as the season turns toward spring, Giles is again needed by the flock:

> And night-fall'n LAMBS require the shepherd's care,
> And teeming EYES, that still their burden bear;
> Beneath whose sides tomorrow's dawn may see
> The milk-white strangers bow the trembling knee;

At whose first birth the pow'rful instinct's seen
That fills with champions the daisied green:
For eyes that stood aloof with fearful eye,
With stamping foot now men and dogs defy.

(96)

So the deaths of spring are balanced with the births of winter and a
vision of the unity of rural life is complete. Simple rural existence,
surprising as it may sometimes be to the uninitiated, offers a
reconciliation of death with future life and offers, too, the possibility
of a vision that can accept present pain or plenty with full knowledge
that it is reasonable to expect joy and want. That this is a great deal
more than the idea of things in their season, I doubt, but that such
an ordered vision of life is better understood and stated in rural than
urban terms, Bloomfield would insist.

The reconciliation of death and life is repeated in miniature when
orphaned lambs are joined with ewes whose new offspring have
died. This adoption is encouraged by the shepherds whose sense of
proper husbandry will also force instinct to yield to the betterment
of the herd by separating twin lambs so that both can gain their
fullest possible size. These acts of man that do oppose or augment
instinct, however, are considered acts that have been measured in
terms of future good and future danger. Giles, for literally the first
time in the course of the poem, is indulged with some moments of
unbridled pride when his flock, the result of this prudent husbandry, passes before his neighbors and onto the village green. It is,
then, careful husbandry based on the knowledge of the past, the
judgment of the present, and the reasonable expectations for the
future, that Bloomfield allows to be praised again. Even in the joy of
the present when Giles speaks the final invocation, the patterned
life which holds all time in the kernel of the present is apparent:

"*Another Spring!*" his heart exulting cries;
"*Another Year!* with promis'd blessings rise! . . .
Eternal Power! from whom those blessings flow,
Teach me still more to wonder, more to know:
Seed-time and *Harvest* let me see again;
Wander the *leaf-strewn* wood, the *frozen* plain:
Let the first Flower, corn-waving Field, Plain, Tree,
Here round my home, still life my soul to *Thee*;
And let me ever, midst thy bounties, raise

An humble note of thankfulness and praise!"—

(98–99)

That the best of rural life has become valuable to Giles, too, is of significance, for the reader who does experience a goodly part of the poem over Giles's shoulder may have been led to the same feeling. And, if he has, then Bloomfield's argument has been successful.

VII *Threatened Beliefs*

Bloomfield's limitations may restrict his artistic scope, yet what he saw happening to what he valued, to the whole rural way of life, and perhaps to some of the fodder for England's grand metaphors, was of epic proportion. His initial awarenesses of this change in rural life appear in *The Farmer's Boy,* and they obviously do not allow him to see on to the final ramifications in English society and English letters. In the pattern of his experience, this change was new. He did, however, see the threat to what he knew and understood, and he felt it necessary to defend his threatened beliefs and loves. His only real authority for discourse was his awareness and his own humble background and experience. The attempt to overcome his limitations, then, was necessary if he was to speak to more than those of like awareness and experience. He had somehow to find what was *usable* in his experience that would be understandable to the widest possible audience. The presentation would require some selectivity; not all of rural life as found in the open-field agricultural system was good. But with the advantages of a patterned life in which he could know the consequences of acts and even things, he chose to assail his limitations by turning inward with his argument.

He turned to the viable, persuasive, and artistic patterns that could be drawn from rural life, and he examined and detailed what he found with such loving intensity that he drew his readers into the world of his experience. There, with the marvelous detail of *The Farmer's Boy,* he created with his art a common ground on which his readers could share his awareness and begin to trust his vision. This ground was bounded by the author's limitations, but for the reader who follows him to it, there are satisfactions and attractions. And the reader who travels into Bloomfield's limited world finds him speaking with great authority and power—a much greater authority and power than Bloomfield could have mustered in a genre he could not control or with subjects that were not his own.

The inward turning direction of Bloomfield's argument becomes more apparent when he is read beside a more traditional author who seeks his common ground somewhere between the audience and himself. Such a common ground could contain shared experience, to be sure, but it could be shaped by the expectations created by working within the tradition of a recognized genre, by classical allusion, and by reference to recognized bodies of knowledge outside the subject and the poetry itself. Such externals are generally absent from Bloomfield's poems. When traditional knowledge such as that of husbandry does appear, it is the very stuff of the poem.

I am suggesting, again, that Bloomfield overcame many of his limitations by accepting them. His argument is given ethical strength when the reader becomes aware that this is a speaker who genuinely knows and loves his subject and who usually does not attempt to argue in terms not authentically his own. Bloomfield is careful to meet those expectations the reader might have for him and to further cultivate his reader's trust. This trust is an absolute requirement for the success of an argument that may appeal first to the reader's emotions, and only then to reason and ethics.

VIII   *Some Conclusions*

The Farmer's Boy is a tolerably good poem. Although its diction is not fully musical to the modern ear and its subject seems at first more quaint than immediate, it can speak to us with power. Its descriptive and narrative beauty place it among the first order of rural poems. The structure may appear to the casual reader at best traditional and at worst a weak echo of Thomson's *Seasons*, but our expectations of a seasonal farm poem are constantly confounded by Bloomfield's skill at transitions, contrasts, reversals, and balances. Structure becomes a source of keen delight, a carefully worked expression of the rhythms and values of rural life. Bloomfield's language is sometimes flawed, especially when he attempts a poetic elevation for which he has no natural resources. However, when his persona is most authentically the rural man and he is sure of his angle of reason, his authoritative voice speaks of his subject with dignity, humor, and sympathy. Finally, the *Farmer's Boy* is Bloomfield's best sustained verse. It is not a model for the study of great prosody; in fact, the simultaneous mention of Bloomfield and prosody leads to apologies about the poet's limited education and experience. But it is generally competent and at spots brilliant. It is rural poetry at its limited best.

CHAPTER 3

The Later Works: Continued Awareness and Final Decline

I Rural Tales, Ballads, and Songs

IF there is a unified critical opinion of Bloomfield's works, it is that the first are the best. One modern critic finds that the first poetry, *The Farmer's Boy*, was surely his best;[1] another finds Bloomfield's next work, *Rural Tales, Ballads, and Songs*, full of "undistinguished poems."[2] More recently, Graham Reed observed that in his later works Bloomfield "succumbed to gentility; he allowed a stilted formalism to suffuse his verse," and that his "most ambitious works were in a characteristically eighteenth-century style."[3] In this there is just enough truth to want correcting. Even Edmund Blunden, who is indeed Bloomfield's foremost modern champion, finds *The Farmer's Boy* to be Bloomfield's greatest poem. The rest, he writes, illuminate it, "but none can rival its tenacious contentment in the bosom of earth. . . ."[4] The careful arguments for rural life and against urbanization, nevertheless, are continued in the later works, and it is evident that Bloomfield continued to be aware of the forces that were reshaping his native ground. If his arguments are less effective, it is less from want of conviction than from a lessening of his powers.

Still, as Rayner Unwin remarks, "*Rural Tales* was very far from being a failure."[5] The *Critical Review* in which Southey had so warmly reviewed *The Farmer's Boy* continued to champion the shoemaker-poet. After conceding the difficulty a poet faces in following a meritorious and successful first book and reviewing several of the pieces in the volume, the writer concludes, "We hope and believe that the success of this volume will equal *The Farmer's Boy*, as we are sure that its merits are not inferior. The manner in which that poem has been received is honorable to the public taste and to the public feeling. Neglected genius has too long been the reproach of England."[6] The *Monthly Mirror* in applauding Bloomfield's refusal to attempt to please the critics characterized the poems as "the easy, lively, and natural effusions of a truly poetical mind, abounding in just observation of village life and manners . . ." and predicted that the volume would please well the "almost innumerable admirers of the Farmer's Boy."[7] *Rural Tales* was, in part, responsible for John Clare's glowing praise of Bloomfield:

> Whatever cause his friends may have to regret the death of the Poet— Fame is not one of them for he dyed ripe for immortality & had he written nothing else but "Richard and Kate" [in *Rural Tales*] that fine picture of Rural Life were sufficient to establish his name as the English Theocritus & the first of Rural Bards in this country & as Fashion (that feeble substitute for Fame) had nothing to do with his exaltation its neglect will have nothing to effect his memory it is built on a more solid foundation & time [one line heavily scored out] will bring its own reward to the "Farmer's Boy."[8]

Since, on the one hand, history has proved Clare very wrong— Robert Bloomfield is not a name to conjure with today—and, on the other, time has not yet brought any real reward to Bloomfield's later poems, is it not possible that Clare completely missed the critical mark too? It is a fair question, but one, I think, that can be answered fairly in the negative. Clare was given to hyperbole whenever Bloomfield's name was mentioned, and he himself might be a fitter candidate to be called best of the rural bards. But there are in Bloomfield's later verse meritorious qualities which will be noted and examined here. These qualities are attached to Bloomfield's awareness of the future of English rural life and the future of her urban and rural art.

Rural Tales is a distinct departure from the conservative meter and sometimes elevated style of *The Farmer's Boy*. The subject is still rural life, but here Bloomfield presents a wider variety of characters, frequently in the social context of the village. Romance, rather naturally limited in his first poem which centered on a twelve-year-old, is here celebrated in several of its aspects. Women figure more prominently in the poems than in *The Farmer's Boy*. And Bloomfield now has a greater freedom of setting in which he can pursue the same emotional arguments presented in his first volume. Of the eighteen pieces in the collection, five are called "ballads," two "tales," and the rest either "songs" or nothing at all.

The first of the pieces, "Richard and Kate: or *Fair-Day*," is called "A Suffolk Ballad" but is not in the conventional ballad meter. Instead, Bloomfield uses alternately rhymed, four-line stanzas all in iambic tetrameter with the general effect of fast movement in the verse. The meter may be one of the devices Bloomfield employs in avoiding the rank sentimentality to which the piece might have been subject. The modern reader, in fact, when apprised of the subject of the narrative, steels himself against an encounter with the maudlin, for the poem presents an old rural couple who totter to the green on fair day to watch their children and grandchildren in the festivities and who come tearfully to bless the assembled young before returning home alone. If read as a whole, however, "Richard and Kate" is an affirmation of rural life and the couple themselves.

Richard urges his aging wife to leave her spinning wheel and walk with him to the green. It is fair day, and more:

> "Have you forgot, KATE, prithee say,
> How many Seasons here we've tarry'd?
> Tis *Forty* years, this very day,
> Since you and I, old Girl, were married!"[9]

A humorous realism immediately appears. Their decision to make the long trek is reached because Kate cut her corns the previous night and now can walk more easily. Although theirs has been a life of cares, none intrude on this summer day. Richard even agrees to avoid long-winded tale telling and his ale at sundown so that Kate will join him.

> "Aye KATE, I wool; . . . because I know,
> Though time has been we both could run,
> Such days are gone and over now; . . .
> I only mean to see the fun."
>
> (R, 2)

Richard's statement echoes the patterned life described in *The Farmer's Boy*, and his quiet acceptance of the limitations of age is a natural result of that life.

So Richard in his Sunday breeches leads his wife across the countryside that Bloomfield knew so well. For the old couple, it is a quiet journey into their own past.

> The day was up, the air serene,

The Firmament without a cloud;
The Bee humm'd o'er the level green;
Where knots of trembling Cowslips bow'd.

And *Richard* thus, with heart elate,
As past things rush'd across his mind,
Over his shoulder talk'd to KATE,
Who, snug tuckt up, walk'd slow behind.

(R, 4)

Again we see that life where the land, the things of rural life, and the force of time could all be felt by common folk to have a natural and positive order as Richard remembers the "sly tricks" they once played on each other near a tree they pass. The tree prompts a different reaction from Kate, revealing her awareness of another part of the natural order:

"'Tis true" she said; "But here behold,
And marvel at the course of Time;
Though you and I are both grown old,
This tree is only in its prime!"

(R, 5)

Bloomfield, aware of the sentimental moralizing half a step beyond her statement, has Richard reply, "Well, Goody, don't stand preaching now; / Folks don't preach Sermons at a FAIR" (R, 6).

Richard has predicted that their ten sons and daughters will all greet them and, when they arrive, his expectation is met in full. Sons, daughters, and grandchildren swarm around them, and the social joys of rural life which Bloomfield praised in *The Farmer's Boy* are again his theme.

The games, "Dicky Races," "more fam'd for laughter than for speed," and the very little ale it takes to mellow old Richard causes him to see his own past in the racers and to feel an almost foolish rejuvenation:

"I'm surely growing young again:
I feel myself so kedge and plump.
From head to foot I've not one pain;
Nay, hang me if I cou'd'nt jump."

(R, 9)

His wife cuts short his fantasy by gently reminding him of his promise to return home at sunset, and tells him the children want time to talk with them. Like a youthful lover he "chuckt her by the chin" and they join the assembled family for a farewell quart of ale. There beneath a tree on the green, the old couple watch their grandchildren play.

Richard, full of a father's pride and the knowledge of his own mortality, utters a simple and emotional speech. A realistic figure capable of stumbling and foolishness yet full of a natural dignity, Richard stands opposed to the stereotype of the loutish peasant:

> "My Boys, how proud am I to have
> My name thus round the Country spread!
>
> Through all my days I've labour'd hard,
> And could of pains and Crosses tell;
> But this is Labour's great reward,
> To meet ye thus, and see ye well."
>
> (R, 11)

There is decorousness in the old man not dwelling on the vicissitudes he has known but being pleased with his humble reward. He tells of his wife's wishes which are sometimes mixed with tears, and of his own assurance to her that life moves as it will, giving man little to do but pray. Richard then pronounces a father's blessing on them all, and the poem moves to its emotional peak. The language is more natural than that which Wordsworth usually manages for his rustics:[10]

> "May you be all as old as I,
> And see your Sons to manhood grow;
> And, many a time before you die,
> Be just as pleased as I am now."
>
> Then (raising still his Mug and Voice,)
> "An Old Man's weakness don't despise!
> I love you well, my Girls and Boys
> God bless you all;" . . . so said his eyes—
>
> For, as he spoke, a big round drop
> Fell bounding on his ample sleeve;
> A witness which he could not stop,
> A witness which all hearts believe.
>
> (R, 12–13)

Only the next, stanza 37, is unfortunate, for Bloomfield slips away from simple language to poetize on filial piety. But he ends the piece simply and satisfyingly enough for the reader to grasp something of the humble fulfillment possible in the country:

> With thankful Hearts and strengthen'd Love,
> The poor old PAIR, supremely blest,
> Saw the Sun sink behind the grove,
> And gain'd once more their lowly rest.
>
> (R, 13)

Another age of rural love is the subject of "Walter and Jane: or, The Poor Blacksmith," which Bloomfield further titles "A Country Tale." The vehicle for the tale is the iambic pentameter in the rhymed couplets of *The Farmer's Boy*, but, perhaps because his intent is less serious here, the couplets are less satisfying. It is here that charges of too strong an affinity with the Augustans are most telling, although Bloomfield does put the couplet to his own unique use. The whole piece, however, is less satisfying than "Richard and Kate."

"Walter and Jane" is the story of a young village blacksmith who falls in love with a pretty country maid just before she leaves the village to move some twelve miles away. The smith's feelings are persistent, and it is not long before he begins walking across the countryside to see her on Sundays. But Walter hesitates to tell her offering for his girl, "conscience" soon causes him to stop his visits offering for his girl, "conscious" soon causes him to stop his visits and fall into gloomy depression. Perhaps because the verse is somewhat ponderous or because there are no clear, realistic pictures to bring the characters to life, the tale, thus far, seems interminable and flat.

After a month of "sharp conflict" within himself, Walter once more sets out to visit Jane. The Sunday bells, the warm day, and the pleasant heath, however, tempt him to rest on a bed of green where his anguished thoughts about poverty again seize him:

> "Why do I go in cruel sport to say,
> 'I love thee Jane, appoint the happy day?'
> Why seek her sweet ingenious reply,
> Then grasp her hand and proffer . . . poverty?
> Why, if I love her and adore her name,
> Why act like time and sickness on her frame?
> Why should my scanty pittance nip her prime,

> And chace away the Rose before its time?
> I'm young 'tis true; the world beholds me free;
> Labour ne'er show'd a frightful face to me;
> Nature's first wants hard labour *should* supply;
> But should it fail, 'twill be too late to fly."
>
> (R, 20–21)

The very real plight of the rural laborer is here, but it is not until this point that Bloomfield himself begins to sound convinced of his subject. Walter continues to muse on his dilemma, recognizing that his love for Jane has become the source of some humor in the village:

> "Oft from my pain the mirth of others flows;
> As when a neighbor's Steed with glancing eye
> Saw his par'd hoof supported on my thigh:
> Jane pass'd that instant; mischief came of course;
> I drove that nail awry and lam'd the Horse;
> The poor beast limp'd: I bore a Master's frown,
> A thousand times I wish'd the wound my own."
>
> (R, 21–22)

The sudden appearance of Jane at the close of his meditation is a bit contrived as is the visit of the young lovers to the cottage of the Widow Hind who counsels them to marry despite the possible hardships.

The advice of the widow is based on her own past experience, but her speech lacks the quiet dignity of the farmer's husbandry lecture to Giles in *The Farmer's Boy.* Walter's reaction, based in part on not wanting to imitate his uncle who lived all his days a bachelor, is to abandon his fears while love "Silenc'd the arguments of Time and Change" (R, 28). Although not an unrealistic potrayal, this still wants the less cluttered handling of events and emotions in "Richard and Kate." The lack of simplicity and delicacy is doubly unfortunate, for not only is the artistry of the piece damaged, but the dependent argument is also weakened.

Aside from his general concern with rural poverty, Bloomfield is preparing to argue for the continuance of the positive relationship between labor and rural wealth that he described at the close of "Summer" in *The Farmer's Boy.* There is an example here for every country squire who might be tempted by the new sensibility that

could divorce him from the people. As Walter finishes his pledge of
love, an unannounced guest enters the cottage:

> Around with silent reverence they stood;
> A blameless reverence . . . the man was good.
> Wealth had he some, a match for his desires,
> First on the list of active Country 'Squires.
> Seeing the youthful pair with downcast eyes,
> Unmov'd by Summer flowers and cloudless skies,
> Pass slowly by his gate; his book resign'd,
> He watch'd their steps and follow'd far behind,
> Bearing with inward joy, and honest pride,
> A trust of WALTER'S kinsman ere he died,
> A hard earn'd mite, deposited with care,
> And with a miser's spirit worshipt there.
>
> > (R, 30–31)

A man who had gained an old laborer's trust, probably by just such
concerned action as the squire took for Walter and Jane, is in
Bloomfield's rural ethic a good man. His concerns are more with
living within the natural order of rural life than with earning money.
The squire presents the couple with the small purse of gold, but
goes beyond that to offer "a spare Shed that fronts the public road"
as a shop for Walter (R, 31).

Wealth held in moderation and administered with benevolence is
the friend of the natural rural order. The action of the squire
parallels the good husbandry of the farmer in Bloomfield's first
work. Both appear to grow from a knowledge of the human and
natural bonds within which rural man must live, and both cultivate
those bonds with more than enlightened self-interest. Both adminis-
ter to man and nature selflessly with an unspoken recognition that
the meaning of rural life lies in mutual trust between man and
nature, hence between man and man. And both know that man's
dignity rests on his striving, his sense of enterprise, which is far
more important than any goal. A casteless concern with the human
condition, then, remains a part of Bloomfield's argument even
though this particular poem lacks his best hand:

> Comforts may be procur'd and want defied,
> Heav'ns! with how small a sum, when right applied!
> Give Love and honest Industry their way,

Clear but the Sun-rise of Life's little day,
Those we term poor shall oft that wealth obtain,
For which th' ambitious sigh, but sigh in vain:
Wealth that still brightens, as its stores increase;
The calm of Conscience, and the reign of peace.

(R, 32)

The poem ends with Walter in his gratitude pledging his support to the squire. It is not simply free horseshoeing and help with harvesting that Walter offers to the squire. The offer promises more than celebrating his good fortune or avenging his wrongs. Walter pledges his friendship as one free man to another, and the offer, although humbly and respectfully made, transcends any hint of caste that would ultimately have detracted from its value.

Bloomfield followed "Walter and Jane" with another tale of rural love, again in iambic pentameter and again in undistinguished form. "The Miller's Maid," although of scant thematic interest, does show Bloomfield to be in better control of the couplet. The tale of two foundlings taken in at different times by a kind village miller and his wife has some familiar echoes. The youngsters fall in love, are next thought to be brother and sister, and are finally freed to marry by the discovery of their true and separate parentages. As if all this is not quite enough, the benevolent miller retires, giving the mill to the newlyweds, and with an old veteran who held the key to their identities as a new addition to the family, they all prepare to live prosperously and happily for a considerable time to come. All of this Bloomfield handles at a sprightly pace and with an enthusiasm that strains to overcome the conventional plot. For the reader who has persevered, this part of *Rural Tales* still promises a bit of charm and honest rustic sentiment.

"The Widow to her Hour-Glass" which follows in the collection may have been one of Bloomfield's more popular pieces, for Hazlitt quotes it easily in his essay "On a Sun-Dial,"[11] and it is a pleasant poem. The stanza approximates the hourglass in printed shape and meter with a final "turning up" of the new stanza as one might turn the glass:

Come, friend, I'll turn thee up again:
Companion of the lonely hour!
Spring thirty times hath fed with rain
And cloath'd with leaves my humble bower,
          Since thou has stood

> In frame of wood,
> On Chest or Window by my side:
> At every Birth still thou wert near,
> Still spoke thine admonitions clear.—
> And, when my husband died,
>
> I've often watch'd thy streaming sand
> And seen the growing Mountain rise,
> And often found Life's hopes to stand
> On props as weak in Wisdom's eyes.

> (R, 59–60)

Perhaps because Bloomfield's own age gives him greater sympathy with his older characters, or because his great love for his own mother is captured here, or because the widow and the hourglass and the whole sad, quiet passing of time best suits his elegiac tone, the firm control and loving execution of detail are present again. His tropes and images are quite plain:

> Its conic crown
> Still sliding down,
> Again heap'd up, then down again;
> The sand above more hollow grew,
> Like days and years still filt'ring through,
> And mingling joy and pain.

> (R, 60)

Simplicity need not be displeasing or unworthy. What claim to artistic merit the poem makes, in fact, comes from that sure, quiet grace of predictability. This is not the crude conventionality of plot that mars the previous tale, but a fair and fond representation of the predictable passing of time and life and things within the greater mutability of the natural order. This is a fair representation, too, of many an aging rural woman's thought and speech; many cultural primitivists in many centuries of art have sought that voice.

There is something in the hourglass, in the object itself, that is predictable and to the widow, almost hypnotic. It is not simply the passing of time that she sees, although she does see that and she does measure her morning by it. When the widow leaves her cottage to glean in the harvest fields, time or the hourglass gets a holiday. The object is idle, of course, but more important is the sense that the past and future suddenly inhabit the timeless present of rural labor. The timeless vision of the plowman in *The Farmer's*

Boy suggests the stopping of time too. It is as if the object, like so many other rural tools and furnishings, is endowed with life and meaning by the seasonal turnings around it. One remembers the tools addressed in *The Farmer's Boy*. The glass is at once a tool and an object for mediation, and the widow's language mixes these functions:

> Steady as Truth, on either end
> Thy daily task performing well,
> Thou'rt Meditation's constant friend,
> And strik'st the Heart without a Bell.

(R, 60)

But when the object prompts the old woman to invoke the seasons which lie within it, it has sufficient power and meaning to accomplish that:

> Come, lovely May!
> Thy lengthen'd day
> Shall gild once more my native plain;
> Curl inward here, sweet Woodbine flow'r;———.

(R, 62)

As she pauses, the object becomes again a thing, a tool, a reality of rural life, and she can address it directly. The marvel of the old widow, of the poem, and perhaps of rural life itself is that the calm, firm tone of her address has, since the first stanza, kept our concern with the timeless present or with the future. The past does not intrude as it might if the widow grasped for it with maudlin attachment. The past is with her in the timeless present of spinning and the hourglass and the seasons, but it is to the new season that she has turned. And as if she affirms the future in the glass, she concludes: "Companion of the lonely hour, / I'll turn thee up again." That surety of vision based on the knowable life appears again. Her attitude differs from stoicism as affirmation differs from acceptance.

"Market Night" which follows in *Rural Tales* has another country woman as speaker. This time, however, the husband is alive and is simply absent one naked winter night. As the wife awaits his return from the distant marketplace, she addresses the spirits of the elements and of his steed, those forces on which his safe journey depend:

> "O WINDS, howl not so long and loud;
> Nor with your vengeance arm the snow:
> Bear hence each heavy-loaded cloud:
> And let the twinkling Star-beams glow."
>
> Now sweeping floods rush down the slope,
> Wide scattering ruin. . . . Star, shine soon!
> No other light my Love can hope—
> . . . .
> O blest assurance, (trusty steed,)
> To thee the buried road is known;
> HOME, all the spur thy footsteps need,
> When loose the frozen reign is thrown."
>
> (R, 63–65)

The uncertainty of the night is broken as the storm moves off to the West and the first star appears. When her husband appears "cloath'd in snow," the reunion is almost anticlimactic. Even the husband's words of counsel that end the piece sound ordinary, as if there was really little to be concerned about:

> "Dear Partner of my nights and days,
> That smile becomes thee! . . . Let us then
> Learn, though mishap my cross our ways,
> It is not ours to reckon when."
>
> (R, 69)

Such homely moralizing is not unrealistic nor, considering the wife's consternation, is it uncalled for. Even the authenticity of a husband persuading his wife to be less the worrier, however, does not rescue the poem from a final flatness. When Bloomfield essays the traditional ballad stanza in "The Fakenham Ghost," flatness is thankfully relieved. A key difference between these two poems is that in the second, Bloomfield returns to artistic preservation of the good in rural life and customs which marked *The Farmer's Boy*.

Founded on an actual incident that Bloomfield heard from his mother, "The Fakenham Ghost" is the passing humorous tale of an ancient dame who thinks that she is being pursued by a ghoul as she walks home at night through Euston Park. The setting is established well enough as she walks quickly by the wooded hillside:

> Where clam'rous Rooks, yet scarcely hush'd

> Bespoke a peopled shade;
> And many a wing the foilage brush'd
> And hov'ring circuits made.
>
> (R, 71)

The ghost is soon heard padding behind the poor creature, and she,
glimpsing the "monster," has her fright increased:

> Regardless of whate'er she felt,
> It follow'd down the plain!
> She own'd her sins, and down she knelt,
> And said her pray'rs again.
>
> (R, 73)

The humor of the piece turns on the discovery that the persistent
specter that follows the old dame through the park gate and to her
cottage steps where she faints is nothing more than an ass's foal
which has lost its dam and has affectionately followed the woman.
Such innocent fun and the years of storytelling that follow such an
incident are a real enough part of rural life. And the verse itself,
which Bloomfield manages with several smooth, realistic touches, is
certainly no worse than a hundred other clever ballads. It was, in
fact, one of Bloomfield's poems which remained quite popular with
children and adults throughout the nineteenth century. What may
be more important, however, is the fact that Bloomfield presents
yet another facet of rural life, and presents it with much the same
humorous fondness that marked several of *The Farmer's Boy*
episodes. Bloomfield disapproved of the rural tendency toward
superstition and chastised it gently in the piece. But the country
love for a good tale that could be retold many times without losing
its freshness is presented as another of Bloomfield's positive values.

"The Fakenham Ghost" is followed by another ballad in the same
verse form as "Richard and Kate." Only the verse form, however,
links this poem to the others, for "The French Mariner" is an
antiwar address by a dying French veteran to the conquering
Britons. The old man tells of the loss of his family and companions
and argues for peace. It is not one of Bloomfield's better poems, for
although peace and an end to "redcoat mania" were dear to him, he
has wondered too far from the source of his poetic power. The
reader need only turn on to "Dolly," which employs the same verse
form and has as its subject a young rustic couple's parting as the boy
goes to war, to find sharper representations of scene and emotion.

If "Dolly" is not the best of Bloomfield's short rural poems, neither is it mere doggerel. Here again Bloomfield handles sentiment in an acceptable and pleasing fashion. The situation itself allows no humor to offset the sadness of the young lovers' parting; instead, Dolly is given the perspective of time and can tell her part of the tale with the quiet resolution and self-awareness possible for the "uneducated" in the knowable life within the natural order. She can know, for instance, that the first pains of parting will be the worst. Her description of her love's horse carrying him away ends in unexpected understatement that affirms her awareness:

> Then down the road his vigour tried,
> His rider gazing, gazing still;
> *"My dearest, I'll be true,"* he cried: . . .
> And, if he lives, I'm sure he will.
>
> (R, 89)

The poem closes with her invocation to the turning seasons and ends, for that, rather well.

"Dolly," then, is one of the poems with relative merit that saves *Rural Tales* from charges of mediocrity. The "elevated" and unsuccessful "Lines, Occasioned by a Visit to Whittlebury Forest" with their unhappy Thomsonian echoes, the uninspired "Song for a Highland Drover," and the occasional piece, "Word to Two Young Ladies," do no such service. Of Bloomfield's three addresses to young ladies, "Nancy," "Rosy Hannah," and "Lucy," the last two have the merits of simplicity and pleasantness and freedom from any false literary tone. Curiously, that tone which also mars "Hunting Song" is absent from "The Shepherd and His Dog Rover" and "Winter Song," and the resulting failure and success of the pieces warrant examination.

Simply stated, the difference between the successful poems and the mediocre or poor ones lies in the voice that the poet chooses. Bloomfield can attempt to speak as "the poet" as he does in "Hunting Song," and the result is hollow, imitative, and strained:

> Ye darksome Woods where Echo dwells
> Where every bud with freedom swells
>   To meet the glorious day;
> The morning breaks; again rejoice;
> And with old Ringwood's well-known voice
>   Bid tuneful Echo play.
>
> (R, 113)

Old Ringwood, even given the handicap of his name, is not an accessible image; he is no more a believable hound than Echo here is a believable sprite. There is no authenticity to the speaker's voice. Any passing poet could have written the lines without having seen a foxhunt. But when in "The Shepherd and His Dog Rover" Bloomfield once more speaks with the voice of the peasant poet, when he is the rural artist with all his strengths and limitations, he can assume the persona of the shepherd and a real countryside and a real dog are there:

> ROVER, awake! the grey Cock crows!
> Come, shake your coat and go with me!
> High in the East the green Hill glows;
> And glory crowns our shelt'ring Tree.
> The Sheep expect us at the fold:
> My faithful Dog, let's haste away,
> And in his earliest beams behold,
> And hail, the source of cheerful day.
>
> (R, 111)

Although this verse is much more exclamatory and emotional, the excitement and joy are justified by half a dozen concrete terms and the easy observation that dogs do shake themselves in the morning. When Echo appears in the second stanza to waft the dog's "gladsome voice" across the fresh fields, there is no straining for a classical spirit to compose itself before the reader at the mention of its name. It is an echo first, simple and real. If the reader wants to move from primal reality to myth, and he probably will not, the transition would be far less strained than is the tired evocation of the myth in "Hunting Song." Bloomfield's language in his better poems is not, of course, without elevation and intensity. It is simply intensified and elevated within the limitations of the rural speaker's voice.

"Winter Song," which closes the volume, catches the right tone and specificity. Bloomfield uses the persona of rural man. The speaker is addressing his son in a speech full of simple morals which, if they are clichés to the modern reader, are so because the kind of life they indicate is no longer enough in our possession to make them urgent and meaningful. Although winter for the poor wears a frightening frown and Bloomfield protests "The silent neglect and the scorn / Of those who have plenty to spare," there remain the simple pleasures of the poor living within the natural order:

> Fresh broach'd is my Cask of old Ale,
> Well-tim'd now the frost is set in;
> Here's Job come to tell us a tale,
> We'll make him at home to a pin.
> While my Wife and I bask o'er the fire,
> The roll of the Seasons will prove
> That Time may diminish desire,
> But cannot extinguish true love.
>
> (R, 117–18)

There are neighborly chats, free from scandal, in which the happenings of the world and the recent sayings of great orators are discussed. As in *The Farmer's Boy*, rural poverty can be protested without weakening the basic appeal of the ordered, knowable life:

> Abundance was never my lot:
> But out of the trifle that's given,
> That no curse may alight on my Cot,
> I'll distribute the bounty of Heaven;
> The fool and the slave gather wealth:
> But if I add nought to my store,
> Yet while I keep conscience in health,
> I've a Mine that will never grow poor.
>
> (R, 118–19)

Without the poem's acknowledgment of rural poverty, this could be a silly, easy optimism. With it, however, the speaker has the dignified voice of rural man cognizant of the freedom and independent enterprise that are his. The sound of stereotyped sentiment may be more the result of modern inapplicability than original triteness, for it is difficult to imagine the urban poor speaking from such a recognizable system of positive values arising from their way of life—from a way of life they can trust.

Rural Tales, Ballads, and Songs, then, is not so fine and even a work as *The Farmer's Boy.* It does contain several good rural poems that recommend it, and if what Claire Blunden calls the "authentic voice of the countryman"[12] is to be valued in our culture, these are worthy of our consideration. Even at his worst, Bloomfield is more pleasing than most of the other "uneducated poets." By saying this I do not mean to damn him with faint praise. If within his own limitations and the limitations of rural poetry he wrote admirably, should he not win approbation? Should criticism demand of a rural writer that he abandon his authentic voice or demand that Milton's pastoral elegy adopt it? I think not. It is more important that Bloomfield's conviction of the merit of his earlier arguments for rural life continues and that he finds at times the right voice and vehicle for those arguments.

II   Wild Flowers; or, Pastoral and Local Poetry

The authentic voice and the awareness of the passing of the rural way of life do not diminish in *Wild Flowers; or, Pastoral and Local Poetry* (1806); in fact, the general quality is as high as that of *Rural Tales*. The poems may suffer less from the chronological and emotional proximity to the writing of *The Farmer's Boy* than those of *Rural Tales*. Too, Bloomfield was further from the shadow of Capel Lofft's influence, and while that fact may have little to do with the poetry in the volume, it does allow Bloomfield more freedom to introduce his own work and to make some of his first public critical utterances.

Although the book is dedicated to Bloomfield's lame son, Charles, and even contains a tale concerning lameness, "The Broken Crutch," it is free from inordinate sentimentalism. The three-page "Dedication," honest and witty prose, is addressed "To My Only Son." "My Dear Boy," it begins: *In thus addressing myself to you, and in expressing my regard for your person, my anxiety for your health, and my devotion to your welfare, I enjoy an advantage over those dedicators who indulge in adulation;—I shall at least be believed.*"[13] Continuing by asserting that he has many friends who deserve to be honored, Bloomfield chooses instead to honor his son and to hope that the book "will be productive of sweets of the worldly kind" that Charles might not be able to win himself. The poet's desire that the book might somehow aid Charles's progress to manhood will not be lost on a sympathetic reader. But as the wish was written during years of relative comfort and its kind seldom repeated in leaner years, I doubt that it was intended as a desperate public appeal for support.

The preface expresses Bloomfield's concern with the tenets of Augustan criticism; in an understated fashion, he reveals himself obedient to them:

A Man of the first eminence, in whose day (fortunately perhaps for me) I was not destined to appear before the public, or to abide the Herculean crab-tree of his criticism, Dr. Johnson, has said, in his preface to Shake-

speare, that—"Nothing can please many, and please long, but just representations of general nature." My representations of nature, whatever may
be said of their *justness,* are not general, unless we admit, what I suspect to
be the case, that nature in a village is very much like nature everywhere
else. It will be observed that all my pictures are from humble life, and most
of my heroines servant maids. Such I would have them: being fully
persuaded that, in no other way would my endeavours, either to please or
to instruct, have an equal chance of success. (W, vii)

Although the passage does reveal Bloomfield to be aware of his
limitations, he is certainly not fawning mindlessly before the dicta of
Dr. Johnson. His quick humor serves him well. Continuing with his
recognition of his own limited range in literature, Bloomfield reveals that he is most pleased to have been "instinctively relished" by
the ladies "who have so decided an influence over the lives, hearts,
and manners of us all" (W, viii). If Bloomfield was indeed following a
conscious course of persuasion, a knowledge of his audience would
be most important. The ladies would, of course, be important, as
would another highly moral segment of the reading public with
whom he dealt by warning of the humor to come in poems:

Perhaps, in some of them, more of mirth is intermingled than many who
know me would expect, or than the severe will be inclined to approve. But
surely what I can say, or can be expected to say, on subjects of country life,
would gain little by the seriousness of a preacher, or by exhibiting fallacious
representations of what has long been termed Rural Innocence.[14]

Such instinctive honesty aided Bloomfield in maintaining the authenticity of his humor. By allowing a bit of the roughness of rural
mirth to come alive, he actually did lose the support of one
influential critic who wanted something more elevated. Although
his voice is authentic and his poetry at least equal to that in *Rural
Tales,* his days of great popularity were ending.

Bloomfield drew less public notice with the issuance of *Wild
Flowers* than with either of his earlier volumes, and some of the
criticism he did receive was less than positive. *The Critical Review*
while finding some merit in these poems hinted that their quality
could not match *The Farmer's Boy* or *Rural Tales:*

Everything new that comes from the pen of a writer so well known to the
public as Mr. Bloomfield, must excite considerable expectation; an expectation, that will be satisfied with nothing beneath the standard of his first

production, and not be a little dissatisfied with the aspect of anything verging to mediocrity. This demand for superior excellence is a tax which merit pays to the public for a due estimation of its value.[15]

The reviewer's "sanguine" expectations for *Wild Flowers* were not met by the poems which he variously finds "tediously told," "heavy and thinly relieved with flowers of either thought or phraseology," and "beneath the standard of either rustic grace or even rustic humour." And he concludes rather harshly:

On the whole, there are several passages in the present volume of very respectable though not transcendent merit. We cannot, however, bestow on it even a general, much less an unqualified degree of approbation. We venture to say that four verses out of five in the average of every poem, are such as would never have ushered Mr. Bloomfield into notice as a first production, and are therefore unworthy of being his last. There is nevertheless imbecility of conception which pervades the whole volume, a mediocrity of spirit which occasionally reaches a pretty thought, but never ventures to one that is bold or energetic.[16]

Wild Flowers begins with a "Familiar Ballad" called "Abner and the Widow Jones." Abner is a plowman who, in order to save his aging horse from becoming food for the hounds, determines to pay court to the Widow Jones whose farm would give both horse and plowman a place to live out their natural days. The seriocomic story is given a bit more interest when the reader discovers that Abner and Mary, the widow, had been in love years before when meddling friends dissuaded her from marrying him. After speaking to her of the past, Abner states his desire with simplicity and practicality:

> "All that's gone by: but I've been musing,
>   And vow'd, and hope to keep it true,
> That she shall be my own heart's choosing
>   Whom I call wife.—Hey, what say you?
> . . . .
> Perhaps that little stock of land
>   She holds, but knows not how to till,
> Will suffer in the widow's Hand,
>   And make poor Mary poorer still."
>
> (W, 5–6)

And if this love and logic might fail to persuade the now tearful

widow, Abner begins a lamentation for the possible fate of old
Bayard:

> "You know poor Bayard; here's the case,—
>   He's past his labour, old, and blind:
> "If you and I should but agree
>   To settle here for good and all,
> Could you give all your heart to me,
>   And grudge that poor old rogue a stall?
> I'll buy him, for the dogs shall never
>   Set tooth upon a friend so true;
> He'll not live long, but I for ever
>   Shall know I gave the beast his due."
>
> (W, 8–9)

After Abner has continued at some length about the character of
the beast, the widow gives "something like consent," consent to at
least stable the horse at her farm. When he arrives home to find that
Bayard is to go to the dogs the following day, Abner determines to
borrow from the widow the money to save him. Next morning the
plowman sets off to see her but turns back realizing that he cannot
bring himself to borrow from her when she is not his wife. The
ensuing scene between farmer and laborer is yet another of
Bloomfield's exempla that portray the best relationship of rural men
and again it is juxtaposed to the proper relationship of man and beast
or man and nature. And so, when the farmer agrees to pay Abner his
wages and sell Bayard to him for a nominal sum, the plowman and
the old horse arrive victoriously at the widow's farm. The plowman's
efforts and sensibility support the natural order in which labor is
rewarded justly, and the poem ends on a didactic note that favors
the rural ethic:

> O Victory! for that stock of laurels
>   You keep so snug for camps and thrones
> Spare us *one twig* from all their quarrels
>   For Abner and the Widow Jones.
>
> (W, 19)

Bloomfield follows with one of his favorite poems. "To My Old
Oak Table" is a serious meditation upon an object which has, for the
poet, been invested with those values and energies that he prized in

rural life. Using the couplet form of *The Farmer's Boy*, Bloomfield shows that he is not limited to descriptive realism when writing respectable verse. When he begins his meditation speaking as the poet, his situation is something like the reverse of Milton's in writing *Lycidas*. Milton, an educated man of letters, speaks through the mask of the ideal shepherd. He is striving neither for strict realism nor for total credibility in his pose. Bloomfield is the untutored genius who, in a sense, adopts the mask of the poet and elevates his song above the humble roughness of country speech. Between real and ideal, both situations create a tension, although Milton's favors the latter and Bloomfield's the former.

The table on which he had composed much of his verse and the emotions and traditions that surround it is the subject; Bloomfield creates a very real object with sufficient import to justify a serious meditation without painting a more particularized picture than the phrase "old oak table" evokes:

> Friend of my peaceful days! substantial friend,
> Whom wealth can never change, nor int'rest bend,
> I love thee like a child. Thou wert to me
> The dumb companion of my misery,
> And oftner of my joys;—then as I spoke,
> I shar'd thy sympathy, Old Heart of Oak!
> For surely when my labour ceas'd at night,
> With trembling, feverish hands, and aching sight,
> The draught that cheer'd me and subdu'd my care,
> On thy broad shoulders thou wert proud to bear.
>
> (W, 21)

The table is a reference point to which the poet can turn for knowledge of his past:

> Thou cam'st, when hopes ran high and love was young;
> But soon our olive-branches round thee sprung;
> Soon came the days that tried a faithful wife,
> The noise of children; and the cares of life.
>
> (W, 22)

Silent companion in the turning seasons and the passing cares of the poet's young family, the table becomes more and more a thing of solidarity as the poet recalls his early struggles. The illness of a child had barely passed when the poet felt the first upheavals in his own constitution:

> Yet Care gain'd ground, Exertion triumph'd less,
> Thick fell the gathering terrors of Distress;
> Anxiety, and Griefs without a name,
> Had made their dreadful inroads on my frame;
> The creeping Dropsy, cold as cold could be,
> Unnerv'd my arm, and bow'd my heat to thee.
>
> (W, 24)

When spring and regeneration come, the strength of the table remains as if it were the very heart of rural man and rural life: resigned, determined, cautiously hopeful.

As the poet's meditation turns from past toward present, he recalls another result of the springtime regeneration and summer's "gay plumes":

> Awaking memory, that disdains control,
> They spoke the darling language of my soul:
> They whisper'd tales of joy, of peace, of truth,
> And conjur'd back the sunshine of my youth:
> Fancy presided at the joyful birth,
> I pour'd the torrent of my feelings forth;
> Conscious of *truth* in Nature's humble track,
> And wrote "The Farmer's Boy" upon thy back!
>
> (W, 27)

The seasonal outline of human life is here again as is the knowable quality of life within the natural order. The future, then, remains for the poet to consider, and he determines to live it with constant reference to the table and its signal qualities:

> The sight of thy old frame, so rough, so rude,
> Shall twitch the sleeve of nodding Gratitude;
> Shall teach me but to venerate the more
> Honest Oak Tables and their guests—the poor.
>
> (W, 28)

And those who could not recognize what enabled them to progress in life would not be his guests nor lean "a sacrilegious elbow" on the table and those qualities and people it represents. At this point the table has become a sacred object, an altar to rural life, and at the same time through personification and skillful generalization Bloomfield gives the reader a sense and feeling for the size and solidarity of the object itself.

"The Horkey, a Provincial Ballad" celebrates the harvest festival. As if to prove that he had a number of voices with which to speak, Bloomfield drops the mask of the meditating poet and writes "to preserve the style of a gossip, and to transmit the memorial of a custom" (W, 31). It is given form and substance by a local tradition which Bloomfield describes in the "Advertisement":

In Suffolk husbandry, the man who, (whether by merit or by sufferance I know not) goes foremost through the harvest with the scythe or the sickle, is honoured with the title of "*Lord*," and at the Horkey, or harvest-home feast, collects what he can, for himself and brethren, from the farmers and visitors, to make a "frolic" afterwards, called "the largess of spending." By way of returning thanks, though perhaps formerly of much more, or of different signification, they immediately leave the seat of festivity, and with a very long and repeated shout of "a largess," the number of shouts being regulated by the sums given, seem to wish to make themselves heard by people of the surrounding farms. And before they rejoin the company within, the pranks and the jollity I have endeavoured to describe, usually take place. These customs, I believe, are going fast out of use; which is one great reason for my trying to tell the rising race of mankind that such were the customs when I was a boy. (W, 31)

In the delightful traditional ballad stanza, Bloomfield argues for the preservation of at least the spirit of the fading rural traditions.

To remind the readers of what is passing, Bloomfield frames the zesty tale with the awareness that its teller is now dead, but in the telling both she and her tale are quite alive. The speaker is Judie Twitchet, then an old woman and the "Queen of knitters," who can knit a whole worsted sock in the time she takes to tell the story. She was a real woman, Bloomfield's note insists, who lived with his mother's cousin in Honington.

She begins at a merry pace. The women are preparing the feast for the workers who appear before the women's clatter has rightly been stilled:

> "Home came the jovial *Horkey load,*
>   Last of the whole year's crop;
> And Grace amongst the green boughs rode
>   Right plump upon the top.
>
> This way and that the waggon reel'd,
>   And never queen rode higher;
> *Her* cheeks were colour'd in the field,

And ours before the fire."

(W, 37)

The full stacks of victuals and kegs of beer disappear with breathtaking speed, and the evening's fun begins:

> Now all the guests, with Farmer Crouder,
>   Began to prate of corn;
> And we found out they talk'd the louder,
>   The oftner pass'd the Horn.
>
> Out came the nuts; we set a cracking;
>   The ale came round our way;
> *By gom,* we women fell a clacking
>   As loud again as they.

(W, 39)

Songs and jokes lead to the "largess of spending." As the men, full of ale and joy, dash out to *"hallo largess"* beneath the moon, some of the women follow and pin their coattails together. This stirs a spirited chase and the women who are caught willingly forfeit a kiss. Of the chases, "The best fun by half / "Was Simon after Sue":

> "She car'd not, light or dark, not she,
>   So near the dairy door
> She pass'd a clean white hog, you see,
>   They'd *kilt* the day before.
>
> High on the *spirket* [an iron hook] there it hung,—
>   'Now Susie—what can save ye?'
> Round the cold pig his arms he flung,
>   And cried, 'Ah! here I have ye!' "

(W, 44)

The laughter and pranks continue half the night until all find their way home, shouting across the morning damp meadows. As Judie's tale and yarn run out, Bloomfield turns the moral sharply and simply to end the frantic motion of the ballad:

> Poor Judie!—Thus Time knits or spins
>   The worsted from Life's ball!
> Death stopt thy tales, and stopt thy pins,
>   —And so he'll serve us all.

(W, 49)

Predictable as such an ending might be, the reader still meets it with a goodly measure of surprise when he is tipped out of the merriment and quickness of the ballad.

The good fun and romance of this ballad are repeated in "The Broken Crutch." The more fortuitous use of the couplet that marked Bloomfield's earliest work is reflected in the tale of a poor but beautiful country maid who eventually marries a wealthy young member of the gentry. The tale repeats several of the themes and concerns of *The Farmer's Boy*, and it is most natural that Bloomfield again works his emotional arguments for maintaining the old order. There is one notable difference, however; the good rural life is here pictured as completely of the past. The worries and wishes of the poet as parent resonate throughout.

The tale begins with Peggy Meldrums taking leave of her family to become a serving girl as her mother before her had done. Her father, John, now lame and on crutches, is unable to walk the full way with her to her new employment, and his brother Gilbert is helping the girl transport her few belongings. As Peggy and her uncle take leave of her father behind a tangled hawthorn bush, he gives some simple words of moral instruction to the maid which are, of course, overheard by young Herbert Brooks, the wealthy young gentleman. When Herbert passes the comely girl and her uncle on the road, he is enthralled by her beauty. Fortunately, but unknown to her family, his intentions from that moment forth are highly honorable.

Before he can proceed to the romance, however, Bloomfield speaks as the poet and intrudes on the narrative digressing on what the argument printed atop the page calls "Regret for Devastation by Enclosures." The setting is his native countryside, an enchanted place:

> And ever will be, though the axe shall smite
> In Gain's rude service, and in Pity's spite,
> Thy clustering alders, and at length invade
> The last, last poplars, that compose thy shade:
> Thy stream shall then in native freedom stray,
> And undermine the willows in its way,
> These, nearly worthless, may survive the storm,
> This scythe of desolation call'd "Reform."
> No army past that way! yet they are fled,
> The boughs that, when a school-boy, screen'd my head:
> I hate the murderous axe; estranging more

The winding vale from what it was of yore,
Than e'en mortality in all its rage,
And all the change of faces in an age.

(W, 55)

The small changes in farms and village that each succeeding generation make would not, of course, trouble the poet, for they are a part
of the natural order. Bloomfield speaks of a more profound physical
change in the landscape, something more than the loss of a few trees
that would upset his nostalgia. In many cases, enclosure altered the
entire face of a valley or manor bringing rectangular boundaries
where none had been and turning the road system out to serve
external markets rather than in to connect inhabitants.[17] Reform
with its enclosure that separated the worker from his land and the
rural classes from their common ground on the land is the greatest
single force against which the poet had to argue. Cognizant of the
possible audience reaction to his strong objections, Bloomfield
closed the digression thusly:

"Warmth," will they term it, that I speak so free?
They strip thy shades,—thy shades so dear to me!
In Herbert's days woods cloth'd both hill and dale;
But peace, Remembrance! let us tell the tale.

(W, 55–56)

But he returns to his objections by reminding his readers that
Herbert's moated hall is gone: "Its name denotes its melancholy fall,
/ For village children call the spot 'Burnt-Hall' " (W, 56).

Obviously, then, young Herbert Brooks represents certain qualities that the poet regrets seeing pass in the landed gentry, and an
examination of the rest of the tale reveals them clearly. Herbert is
kind, benevolent, honest, and honorable, and free from any artificial
concern with class distinction. When in this rural society where
each man knew his neighbor, he sees Peggy in church, his ardor is
strengthened even more, and he soon meets her on a footbridge and
proposes marriage with a full and considered knowledge of her
humble ancestry. His speech reviews the state of his fruitful lands
and gardens and ends in a simile that has him, like Adam, in need of
a helpmeet.

When Meg accepts, some of her neighbors suspect the worst—
that she will be taken advantage of and ruined. But Herbert is no
urban libertine; plans for the wedding progress. When word of the

match reaches old John Meldrums, it is to him unbelievable. Afraid for his daughter's happiness and honor, the old man rages, banging his crutch against a stile and breaking off the tip. At old John's request Gilbert sets off to defend Meg's honor with the tip of the broken crutch tucked under his coat to use as a cudgel. He arrives at the manor house after the marriage has taken place, and the reader learns that Herbert had sent a cart, unfortunately piloted by a servant full of wedding-ale, to fetch the two old men. There is a good laugh for all when the broken crutch falls out of Gilbert's coat and he must explain that it was his intention to thump Herbert with it. Finally, with old John belatedly fetched by the tipsy servant and all the characters assembled, the tale ends with the father's wish that the poor not be disdained simply because they are poor.

The marriage which defies caste joins two of the kinds of people who once shared rural life. The reader whose sympathies have been caught by the young couple is invited to extend those sympathies to the proper union of these peoples. Class differences are not denied in the final speeches of John and young Herbert; the differences are transcended. This recognition of the mutual humanity, mutual need, and mutual affection of rural folk is a key part of the life for which Bloomfield argues, and this tale, too, illuminates the final lines of "Summer" in *The Farmer's Boy.*

The country, rural life, the natural order, became the conscious source of Bloomfield's strength, both emotional and physical. His flights from London's smoke and crowds in search of that strength are recorded in "Shooter's Hill." This meditation upon health and the life of the artist shares the distinctly antiurban bias that is either stated or implied in a great number of his other poems:

> Aye, there's the scene![18] beyond the sweep
>   Of London's congregated cloud,
> The Dark-brow'd wood, the headlong steep,
>   And valley-paths without a crowd!
> Here, Thames, I watch thy flowing tides,
>   Thy thousand sails am proud to see;
> But where the *Mole* all silent glides
>   Dwells Peace—and Peace is wealth to me
>
>   (W, 79)

His agitation was caused in part by an illness that threatened to keep him from the proposed excursion down the Wye that would become the subject of his next volume.[19] It ends with the poet's resolve to use his knowledge of the past, his rural past, to escape the dangers of vanity and establish a virtuous life. As with the less successful "Visit to Ranelagh" which follows in Bloomfield's text, it is yet another example of those values common to rural poetry. One note, however, about the pictorial quality of the poem should be made. The dark wood, the plunging steep, and the "valley-paths without a crowd" are images that give us the flavor of pre-enclosure countryside and which hint of but do not follow fully the techniques of the sublime. Most important is Bloomfield's image of the valley. It does not contain the fences, the hedge-rows, the roads—in general the imposed order of commercial organization—that followed enclosure. Instead, Bloomfield choses to see "valley paths without a crowd," a distinctly open rural image possible only with the less organized open-field agriculture. Nevertheless, too much could be made of the point, for the picture is not fully drawn here, and Bloomfield's poems are not so rich in pre- and post-enclosure images as are John Clare's.[20]

"Love of the Country" celebrates rural life as the source of truth, reason, intellectual fire, even religious sentiment. It is, artistically, a far different kind of poetry from the rural song, "The Woodland Hallo," that follows it. The former has the more general language of a poet's meditation, while the song, the latter, takes its freshness and joy from the peculiarities of a country voice. These modes are happily joined in "Barnham Water," in which the poet speaks directly of a rural scene. These short pieces with the less successful "Mary's Evening Sigh" are the last of the poems originally published in *Wild Flowers*. The volume ends with the smallpox poem "Good Tidings; or News From the Farm," which had been published separately in 1804.

III   *The Smallpox Poem*

"Good Tidings" is an important poem for an "uneducated" rural man to be making in the early 1800s. While many supposedly more sophisticated men were indulging in unchecked and sometimes hysterical superstition, Bloomfield reveals himself to possess an understanding of at least this area of medical science and to have an enlightened concern for humanity. The poem does suffer from the sound of occasional verse, but Bloomfield's strong feelings for his topic and his good sense in using familiar material make it an interesting piece of didactic writing.

The poem does provide a glimpse of Bloomfield structuring yet another emotional argument. Again he uses a voice his readers would find both easy to sympathize with and authoritative. Using his personal knowledge and suffering he placed his discussion of the disease within the frame of "domestic incident" where his authority lay (W, 106). His argument is a more immediate and direct one than that in *The Farmer's Boy*, for there is a simple, obvious, and specific course of action to be advocated in the use of the vaccine.

Bloomfield begins directly with a pathetic picture of a child blinded early in life, and when the portrait is full enough to warrant some sympathy from the reader, he reveals the cause to be smallpox. In answer to a sympathetic question from the poet's persona the child's mother speaks its history. Her tale ends with a selfless wish: "God keep smallpox from your door" (W, 111), and the poet is freed to ask more questions of the reader. If there were a way to stop the destruction of the horrid disease, to prevent the recurrence of such misery, would the world not rejoice? The day, Bloomfield insists, is present, and he begins by describing the vaccine as another unsuspected treasure of the mean and kine of England's rural reaches. With a brief history of the discovery of the vaccine as another unsuspected treasure of the mead and kine of various cultures throughout history and finds it quite unlike the results of war:

> Twas thine, while victories claim'd th' immortal lay,
> Through private life to cut thy desperate way;
> And when full power the wondrous magnet gave
> Ambition's sons to dare the ocean wave,
> Thee, in their train of horrid ills, they drew
> Beneath the blessed sunshine of Peru.

(W, 117)

Recognizing that this is not his strongest voice, he continues, "But why unskill'd th' historic page explore? / Why thus pursue thee to a foreign shore?" Bloomfield promptly returns to domestic incident.

At the end of the history of an English epidemic, Bloomfield reveals that the victim was his own father. It is a very personal appeal to the readers who valued rural verse. It could, after all, have been the rural bard himself who died. Those who knew and loved his other works are invited now to act on their sympathies to prevent further loss of life (W, 120–22). After writing of his brother Nathaniel, who even as the poem was being written lost a third child to smallpox, Bloomfield moves to more direct questions for his readers. If they love their children and their neighbors, that love can best be shown by protecting them by using the vaccine. After appeals to self-interest and pity, Bloomfield attempts to move his readers with patriotism, for he advocates an English cure that could well be used to cure Englishmen. The strongest of these arguments, however, are those that touch upon the disruption of the rural social order by disease. The self-interest and the respect for a neighbor's safety that might prompt a man to use the vaccine are parts of the responsibility to conserve taught by rural life:

> In village paths, hence, may we never find
> Their youth on crutches, and their children blind;
> Nor, when the milk-maid, early from her bed,
> Beneath the may-bush that embow'rs her head,
> Sings like a bird, e'er grieve to meet again
> The fair cheek injur'd by the scars of pain.
>
> (W, 131)

As this scene is completed, the air of things as they should be returns:

> Pure, in her [the milkmaid's] morning path, wher'er she treads,
> Like April sunshine and the flow'rs it feeds,
> She'll boast new conquests; Love, new shafts to fling;
> And Life, an uncontaminated spring.
>
> (W, 132)

Although this is not Bloomfield at his best, it is the rural writer in a surprisingly good attempt at epideictic discourse on a general and scientific theme. The greatest import of the verse may be a social one, for Bloomfield in 1804 and again in 1806 was not without influence on his large London audience.

IV *Travel Verse:* The Banks of the Wye

The four books of *The Banks of the Wye; A Poem* close Bloomfield's most productive period. He was well aware of the fact that the subjects supplied him by "a short excursion down the Wye, and through part of South Wales" (B, v) would mark a change in his verse. What he was not aware of was that although he records some charming pictures and seeks variety in the changing scene and varied rhythm of the poem, his most authoritative poetic voice is replaced by that of the visitor. The sadly missing ingredient in the poem is, I think, the sense of moral urgencies that shaped the argument of *The Farmer's Boy* and inspired the loving treatment of his subjects in the better short poems. It is Bloomfield's England that he writes about in *The Banks of the Wye*, but however much he loved the experience of the excursion, it is not his in the sense that the farms and villages of Suffolk were his. His understanding of the rural life that linked him to the land and the folk could not be tapped with any regularity in such a travel piece. The images and scenes bombard him from each side, each replete with meaning, tradition, and perhaps beauty of its own. But there is not the continuity of rural life, seasonal change and timelessness, or the natural order, to bind up his experience and make it authentic.

There is a great sadness in the fact that Bloomfield, once he had found a place to stand which lends great authenticity to his point of view, could not take that ground with him and use it to order and interpret a multifarious reality. It is sad to lose any authentic voice, and the authentic voice of the countryman is no exception. Bloomfield's inability to bring with him his ordered vision, his value system, and his rooted knowledge of life does not signal the general impossibility of such an event. The poet was farther removed from his rural experience, his youthful powers, and source of joy than ever before. There are moments in *The Banks of the Wye* when his voice seems sure again—moments usually connected to a flash of passing scenery in which the poet could naturally stand.

> A troop of gleaners chang'd their shade,
> And 'twas a change by music made;
> For slowly to the brink they drew,
> To mark our joy, and share it too,
> How oft, in childhood's flow'ry days,
> I've heard the wild impassion'd lays
> Of such a group, lays strange and new,
> And thought, was ever song so true?
> When from the hazel's cool retreat,
> They watch'd the summer's trembling heat;
> And through the boughs rude urchins play'd,
> Where matrons, round the laughing maid,
> Prest the long grass beneath! And here
> They doubtless shar'd an equal cheer;
> Enjoy'd the feast with equal glee,
> And rais'd the song of revelry:

Yet half abash'd reserv'd, and shy,
Watch'd till the strangers glided by.

(*B*, 18–19)

Even here, however, there is more distance between the artist and his subject than is usual in Bloomfield's verse. In part it is the result of Bloomfield's situation as a tourist, a visitor, and much of it is the lack of particularization that gave life to the meaner objects of rural life in his earlier verse. Unwin's observation that this much re-worked poem was filled with the "spirit of the topographer—the guidebook writer rather than the poet—" is not unfair,[21] and there are not enough of the good scenes to fully redeem the work.

Bloomfield simply fails to take those flights of fancy to give his reader real visions of the past—visions that "The Horkey" proves he could give. A few of the historical sights—the home of "The Man of Ross"—are of interest for themselves, but few of them are made to seem at all important in the way that Bloomfield gives importance to his simple rural histories.

V *Final Labors, Lessened Powers*

Eleven full years elapsed before Bloomfield published another volume of verse. They were not the totally empty and nonproductive years that some studies envision, but Bloomfield, who was past fifty-six, could no longer write at his earlier pace. *May Day with the Muses* may be a long and elaborate exercise in wish fulfillment for the aging poet, for its subject is the acceptance of verse for rent money by an aging baronet whose love of poetry and of his rural neighbors led him to give rural bards their due. From patronage of this kind Bloomfield could have benefited hundreds of times during his career. The death of the old duke of Grafton seemed to end any hope of such enthusiastic assistance.

May Day with the Muses is a poetic frame tale in which all the folk of Oakly manor gather on May Day to present the poems that the eighty-year-old baronet has announced that he will accept as payment for their property rental. The quality of the verse is, after the disappointments of *Banks of the Wye*, surprisingly high. While not so good as *The Farmer's Boy* or the best poems in *Wild Flowers*, this is not the worst of Bloomfield's verse. That the aging poet should, despite illness, poverty, partial blindness, and great depression still be capable of some rather enjoyable poetry may be explained by the

simple fact that he returned to his native ground. At times the frame
verse in his familiar iambic pentameter couplets exceeds the quality
of the songs and ballads themselves; it is good to know that one is
listening to Robert Bloomfield again and listening to him as he
speaks with a sense of who he is.

The poet begins intensely and personally:

> O for the strength to paint my joy once more!
> That joy I feel when Winter's reign is o'er;
> When the dark despot lifts his hoary brow,
> And seeks his polar-realm's eternal snow.
> Though black November's fogs oppress my brain,
> Shake every nerve, and struggling fancy chain;
> Though time creeps o'er me with his palsied hand,
> And frost-like bids the stream of passion stand.[22]

Invoking spring that rejuvenates rural life, he is soon about the
business of introducing Sir Ambrose Higham, the baronet who is
living out his days and taking all his pleasure in the life of Oakly
Hall. Bloomfield's first themes are awakened by the portrait of this
reasonable old gentleman who has said a final good-bye to the strife
and discord of the city to "calmly wait the hour of his decay, / The
broad bright sunset of his glorious day" (M, 5) on his native ground.
Sir Ambrose has the proper attitude toward the rural poor and the
laborers; he is capable of what Bloomfield found in the duke of
Grafton, condescension in its noblest aspect, bringing succour to the
hunger of the children, the loneliness of the old, and the simple
desires of the plowman. His announcement of the verse for rent
agreement is sent to his "neighbors," as he calls everyone in the
manor. The instructions limit the subjects fit for verse by excluding
stupid superstition (bloody ghosts, but not harmless fairies), vulgar
things, and the gothic concerns of crimes, blood, monk's retreats,
magic caverns, and midnight darkness.

Such an offer would in reality meet with reactions varying from
joy to incredulity, and Bloomfield portrays them all. Most important, however, is the effect on the laboring folk of the manor:

> Now shot through many a heart a secret fire,
> A new born spirit, an intense desire
> For once to catch a spark of local fame,
> And bear a poet's honourable name!
> Already some aloft began to soar,

And some to think who never thought before.

(*M*, 10)

Naturally, not all are capable of the feat: "But O, what numbers all their strength applied, / Then threw despairingly the task aside / With feign'd contempt, and vow'd they'd never tried" (*M*, 11). And there are humorous interruptions to the flow of the rural occupations when the would-be bards lose themselves in composing. Spring does finally arrive, and the preparations for the festival of verse are happily drawn by the poet. This time, however, the things the poet values are completely of the past. He neither hesitates to emphasize that fact (*M*, 14–15), nor when lord and labor exchange toasts, does Bloomfield fail to recall part of what he blamed for the destruction of rural life:

> Avaunt, Formality! thou bloodless dame,
> With dripping besom quenching nature's flame;
> Thou cankerworm, who liv'st but to destroy,
> And eat the very heart of social joy;—
> Thou freezing mist round intellectual mirth,
> Thou spell-bound vagabond of spurious birth,
> Away! Away! and let the sun shine clear,
> And all the kindnesses of life appear.

(*M*, 16)

Only in the days before the advent of the detested false refinement could this entertainment and casteless intercourse have happened.

First of the poems to be offered is written by Philip, the farmer's son. The ballad, "The Drunken Father," is an undistinguished temperance poem containing most of the standard features of any temperance piece before or since: the drunken father, the long-suffering wife, the innocent children who go off to the tavern to fetch home their father, and even the miraculous character reversal in which the poor chap takes the pledge. Its most praiseworthy feature is the fact that it moves quickly.

A few lines of transition lead to the next song which has been composed by the gamekeeper of Oakly. "The Forester" is one of the better poems in the collection. In this meditation on the eternal face of Nature, a central feature is a fallen oak which becomes the turning point for some moralizing on the states and kingdoms of man. Before the morals are drawn, however, there are some quiet moments reminiscent of the authentic Bloomfield:

From every lawn, and copse, and glade,
    The timid deer in squadrons came,
And circled round their fallen shade
    With all of language but its name.
Astonishment and dread withheld
    The fawn and doe of tender years,
But soon a triple circle swell'd,
    With rattling horns and twinkling ears.

Some in his root's deep cavern housed,
    And seem'd to learn, and muse, and teach,
Or on his topmost foliage browsed,
    That had for centuries mock'd their reach.

(*M*, 42–43)

That the lines on the fallen oak are a response to the young duke of Grafton's complaint that Bloomfield's muse had been too long inactive I have already noted.

"The Shepherd's Dream" which follows has little to recommend it. "The Soldier's Home," however, deserves at least a moment's notice. An old veteran's tale of returning to his rural cottage gives the reader a sense of the nonlinear time that marks the knowable rural life. The force of the familiar strikes the soldier as he crosses his father's farm to call his father's name at the cottage door. When no one answers, his reaction is not the expected one of fear or grief, "But an o'erpowering sense of peace and home, / Of toils gone by, perhaps of joys to come" (*M*, 58). Once inside the hut, the present and the past are one. He can breathe the cooler air, "And take possession of my father's chair" (*M*, 58), where, perhaps too obtrusively, his initials have survived forty years' wear. The recognition of things, of the familiar ticking clock, however, is to be expected. The appearance of a robin that could not possibly have lived the twenty years of his absence but nevertheless appears to renew an old friendship does suggest the timelessness of life in which the veteran can still find a common ground between the present, his past, and his future.

Bloomfield's disgust with war appears in the old man's raging against its cost and waste. Implicit is his distrust of another system of values alien and hostile to his own. Too, war and its celebration are not within his poetic range. Even the veteran's prologue expresses that recognition:

My untried muse shall no high tone assume,
Nor strut in arms;—farewell my cap and plume:
Brief be my verse, a task within my power,
I tell my feelings in one happy hour.

(*M*, 57)

The mask of the veteran through which the poet speaks imposes further limitations on songs of valor, but these limitations do not obscure the fact that Bloomfield prefers his rural muse.

One of Bloomfield's favorite images, a parade of rural maidens, follows the veteran's song. Their invitation to the dance gives a moment of youthful joy to Sir Ambrose and forms the transition to the introduction of Philip, a rural swain whose intended has been ill, delaying their wedding for a considerable time. "Rosamond's Song of Hope" is her offering; it lacks any of the saving graces of Bloomfield's best poetry. The ballad is followed by "Alfred and Jennet," the last and in some ways the best of the selections.

In the preface to *May Day with the Muses*, Bloomfield writes, "I will plead no excuses for any thing which the reader may find in this little volume, but merely state, that I once met with a lady in London, who, though otherwise of a strong mind and good information, would maintain that 'it is impossible for a blind man to fall in love.' I always thought her wrong, and the present tale of 'Alfred and Jennet' is written to elucidate my side of the question" (*M*, vii). The romantic and sentimental tale told by a sturdy yeoman who is Jennet's father returns to the theme of the proper relationship between labor and the landed within rural society, and for a final time the social barriers are broken—broken by youthful love. Although not far beyond Bloomfield's usual apolitical approach, the blindness of Alfred who represents the gentry has almost inescapable overtones.

The youngsters who grow slowly to love each other are a surprisingly well-matched pair. Jennet is a lively, determined, and lovely girl. Poor as her family is she is not at all a rude rustic; formed by the natural order, her character has two delightful sides:

Her lively spirit lifted her to joy;
To distance in the race a clumsy boy
Would raise the flush of conquest in her eye,
And all was dance, and laugh, and liberty.
Yet not hard-hearted, take me right, I beg.

> The veriest romp that ever wagg'd a leg
> Was Jennet; but when pity soothed her mind,
> Prompt with her tears, and delicately kind.
> The half-fledged nestling, rabbit, mouse, or dove,
> By turns engaged her cares and infant love;
> And many a one, at the last doubtful strife,
> Warm'd in her bosom, started into life.

(M, 74)

Alfred, the blind only child of a wealthy widow, escapes the faults of character that he might have suffered in an overly indulgent or overly protective family and society:

> But Alfred was a youth of noble mind,
> With ardent passions, and with taste refined;
> All that could please still courted heart and hand,
> Music, joy, peace, and wealth, at his command.

(M, 75)

The providence that took his sight replaced it with an inordinate fondness for all that grows in the fields around his home. His explorations of the country immediately around his home are shared by Jennet.

When winter separates the youngsters and Alfred grows gloomy, Jennet is sent for—"just for company"—and is allowed to study with Alfred's governess. The winter passes happily with Alfred at his piano and Jennet listening and talking. The charm of her singing voice, however, she hides from Alfred until he discovers its fame through her father. Finally hearing her songs, Alfred decrees that she will go home no more but remain as his constant companion. So music and poetry, Nature and conversation come to bind them more obviously in love. Alfred's jealousy of the gardener who tries to talk to Jennet convinces her father that they are in love, and he feels morally bound to reveal the fact to Alfred's mother, the proper judge of the situation.

Jennet's tearful return home seems to signal the end of the romance. Alfred's mother, however (and herein lies the moral), does not rule against love. Jennet's returning home is her own response to what she took to be the lady's discomfort. In such a tale when it seems that a character's natural sensitivity and goodness will bring unhappiness, it is customary, to say the least, to have the course of events reversed and pluck joy out of the worst possible mess:

> Down the green slope before us, glowing warm,
> Came Alfred, tugging at his mother's arm;
> Willing she seem'd, but he still led the way,
> She had not walk'd so fast for many a day;
> His hand was lifted, and his brow was bare,
> For now no clust'ring ringlets wanton'd there,
> He threw them back in anger and in spleen,
> And shouted "Jennet" o'er the daisied green.
> Boyish impatience strove with manly grace
> In ev'ry line and feature of his face.
>
> (*M*, 91)

And joy there is when Alfred claims Jennet for his bride; love foils the force of caste, and the gardener who has been quite fond of Jennet is discovered to be too old to die for love.

A touch of Bloomfield's old powers must have survived through this writing. As in many of his other poems, what sentiment is there need not be forgiven, only recognized as part of the authentic rural voice. There are defects in the work that can and should be faulted, however. Although Bloomfield attempts to recapture some of the vibrant reality of the country in the frame to his tales, he does not ultimately succeed. The pictorial quality, so delicate and persuasive in earlier works, is remembered by the artist, but twice in this single work he falls back on the unsatisfactory device of telling the reader that his pictures are as this or that artist would fashion them. The verse itself is uneven and the voice not always true. And if Bloomfield stubbornly grasps his old awarenesses, it is with an unsteady hand.

The aging poet's hope and sense of the dignity of the attempt were not gone, but even these personal qualities were shaken. It is possible that he lost strength at the end of the work or that the publisher lost faith. Several of the poems that he mentions in the closing lines of the frame were real poems that appeared in *The Remains* but which were not published as part of *May Day*. If he knew, and I suspect that he did, that these verses were not strong enough to revive his reputation, then the appeal of his preface was the proper one. "The remembrance of what is past" does include *The Farmer's Boy*, *Rural Tales*, and *Wild Flowers*. That recent years have found few champions for Robert Bloomfield is no indication that there is no remembrance for him, for the verse of the peasant poets, John Clare and others, does remember him. And there is a real possibility that the popularity of Wordsworth and the other romantics, with their rural tales and images drawn from the English countryside, was in part the result of a vast audience whose appetite for such things was whetted by the writings of the farmer's boy.

CHAPTER 4

Bloomfield and the Rural Tradition: Its Value and Values

I The Poet Himself

FROM the biography and poetry of Robert Bloomfield comes a picture of the man. It is possible that we may learn from him, for he is a man whose work is our past and hence a part of our inventive possibilities. From his writings, it may be possible to deduce something of the nature of rural poetry, and from both the poetry and the man, it may be possible to gain a further understanding of the ethical values he found in rural life.

One of the first items in the traditional picture of Bloomfield is that he once charmed audiences the size of which many modern poets might covet and that he now enjoys "real 'Augustan peace' beneath the accumulated dust of the years."[1] This might be explained through the coincidence of Bloomfield's verse with Wordsworth's and by saying that the better poet survived, yet that would be to ignore much that is very good and very bad in the poetry of each. Too, recent years have seen rural poets who stand beside Bloomfield, William Bowles and John Clare, emerge in various states of rediscovery, and two of the latest editions of Bloomfield have come in 1971. This picture of a meteoric career, then, may not contain the final disposition of Bloomfield's reputation.

A gentle man, but not without passion and conviction, Bloomfield might be better remembered now had he committed himself to pursuing his convictions more actively in the noise of politics as did Cobbett or by writing of rural life more dramatically as did Crabbe in his darker verse. His acceptance of political realities and optimistic vision of the life of labor cause the modern and Marxist critic (see Raymond Williams's *The Country and the City*) to feel that excuses

133

must be made for the poet. Bloomfield spoke in ballad, however, not broadside; he argued with celebration, however sad, not dark criticism.

The limited legend that survives Bloomfield is in other ways inaccurate. Although it has been rumored often, it is doubtful that alcohol ruined him. An entry in Crabbe's journal which was appended as a note to *The Village* asserts that Bloomfield had better remained a farmer's boy or a cobbler and not become a poor and unhappy poet. "By the way," Crabbe wrote, "indiscretion did much."[2] By reading no farther, one might guess that the drunkenness and dissipation against which Bloomfield was so often warned by his friends (usually with the "unhappy fate of Burns" as the example) were indeed his errors. But although he was fond of ale and port, a single sodden evening produced such feelings of foolishness and pain that it is difficult to imagine Bloomfield as an habitual drunkard. Crabbe, in fact, did recognize Bloomfield's true indiscretion, but few critics bother to complete the quotation from Crabbe. "It might be virtuous and affectionate in him to help his thoughtless relations; but his more liberal friends do not love to have their favours so disposed of," wrote the parson, adding, "He is, however, to be pitied and assisted." To this excess of generosity in our picture of Bloomfield might be added a final fault: a surfeit of hope for financial success.

A memoir of the poet's life affixed to an 1835 edition of his works furthers the legend of Bloomfield's melancholy disposition, indicating that in his last years, his sanity was feared for. To be sure, as Unwin has remarked, Bloomfield suffered from hypochondria, but that "a morbid interest in his own health dominate[s] his correspondence"[3] is not so sure a thing. The letters do reveal a man in pain, but the presence of just anger, light humor, and a great compassion for his family seems to balance his interest in his own health.

That quitting London for his final home in Shefford failed to renew his spirit and make him once again the farmer's boy is true. The legend and reality are one. The reasons for the unsuccessful return to rural life, however, have not been satisfactorily explicated.

An essentially rural man with rural sensibilities and values, Bloomfield's angle of vision came from his standing place within the natural order of the open-field system of agriculture. His beliefs, his value system, grew naturally from that kind of life that may be even older than the manorial system—a "communal organization of the peasantry, a village community of share-holders who cultivated the land on the open-field system and treated the other requisites of rural life as appendant to it."[4] It was the land itself that bound such a society together. That land (some set apart by tradition and law for the mutual use of all the folk of the manor) was at the heart of Bloomfield's ethical and poetic concerns. The society built on the common dependence on the land, however, had long been threatened by change, for it was seen as an obstacle to economic growth.[5]

What such a tradition and system of governance insured was the right of cottager, laborer, or squatter to obtain a living from the land. The rather complex system of rights and privileges could work to the general advantage of everyone in the manor. The advantages for labor, and it was with labor that Bloomfield's greatest sympathies lay, are succinctly described in Bovill's *English Country Life:*

> Although the open-field system closed the door to progressive agriculture and increased production, which the Napoleonic wars made a compelling need, it gave every countryman the immense advantage of a stake in the land. Nearly all cottagers had at least a strip or two in the common fields, and the rest at least enjoyed legal or customary rights in the wastes where they could graze cows, horses, sheep, geese, and goats. Thus was the labourer able to produce both cheap food for himself and a surplus to send to market. The system gave him an opportunity to rise in the world by saving and investing in more stock or more land in the common field. It also left him free to dispose of his labour as he thought fit, as best suited his interests, on his own holdings or, for wages, on that of a larger farmer.[6]

Bloomfield's boyhood on a small but successful farm allowed him to experience the best of life in the manorial system. The changes in that life that he protested in *The Farmer's Boy* were not new. The gradual process of enclosure, the revolution in agricultural techniques, and the influence of urban capitalism had for long years been eroding the nature of the village and farm. In the sixteenth century, enclosure was given a great stimulus by the new practice of farming for a market—a market that based its demands on rising prices and a growing textile industry:

> When commerce increased its profits and the classes engaged in it stepped into a more lavish style of living, the landlord found himself in a world in which he had to make drastic changes if he wished to maintain his social prestige. In feudal times the lord's pomp and state depended on the number and condition of his tenants. As domestic order became more

secure, the command of men counted for less and less; as wealth grew and all classes acquired more expensive habits, the command of money counted for more and more. With a prosperous cloth trade demanding larger supplies of wool, rich profits were to be made by substituting good pasture for poor arable farming in the Midlands.[7]

The changes already embodied the acceptance of urban social values not too different from the false sensibility that Bloomfield protests in the harvest-home section of *The Farmer's Boy*.

To the lasting detriment of Bloomfield's people, the enclosure movement gained momentum and despite the efforts to protect the rights of the peasant in the ordinances of 1682, 1725, 1769, and 1791, the poor were usually made to suffer. When the loss of their ancient rights to the common land was compensated by awarding them small tracts of land of their own, they far too often found themselves unable to meet the legal expenses of enclosure which required surrounding the land with ditches and hedges. The small farmer or cottager was frequently without sufficient capital both to enclose and to carry on. The very poor who were awarded as little as an acre of land and a bit of cash to make up for the loss of their right to graze a cow on the commons found that a cow could not survive on such a small tract. So, like the others, they were usually forced to sell their land.[8]

Passing, then, was what Thomas Bewick called "the poor man's hermitage" where a laborer might maintain himself and his family and keep a cow, some sheep, geese, or, more commonly, a number of hives.[9] It was not, however, enclosure alone that brought this change, for new techniques of husbandry had been discovered that waited only the beginnings of the accelerated enclosure of the eighteenth century to become popular. Not all of the changes in husbandry would be unpopular to a man like Bloomfield. Some of the new techniques could be adapted to the open-field system and used to improve both the ethical quality of husbandry and the quality of life of the rural folk. The old custom of killing off much of a village's cattle at the end of summer, for example, arose because there was too little food available to winter them. Jethro Tull's experiments in husbandry included the raising of turnips for the specific purpose of feeding cattle in the winter. This particular innovation was practiced on Mr. Austin's farm and is described with approval in *The Farmer's Boy*. Bloomfield's acceptance of such an innovation might be based both on the better economy it afforded in dispensing with the old pattern of feast and famine that had characterized the country life and on the more humane type of husbandry the innovation allowed. However, those techniques, which were dependent upon the economic control of large portions of the land by a single proprietor who would then displace the poor while increasing the production of the land, were not a part of the order Bloomfield revered.

It was finally something like the substitution of "capitalistic farming for the old peasant economy" that ended the order that Bloomfield loved.[10] The action of the English aristocracy in supporting enclosure and capitalistic farming, both of which insured the dependency of the laborer on an employer-owner as opposed to his earlier dependency on the land, was neither without public spirited design nor free from selfish interest. The demand for produce made by the growing cities was resisted by the old system of cooperative control of the land, of common fields, and of widely distributed property rights. Bloomfield himself in *The Farmer's Boy* inveighed against the demands of the city while supporting the old order that gave independence to the rural laborer. At one point in 1802 Bloomfield was "dreaming with a vengence [*sic*]" of buying what was Honington Green to "throw it open" again and erect there a pedestal honoring the rural muse.[11] Writing to a Mr. Pratt who had sent him a poem on "Bread" that vindicated the cottager, the poet wrote, "To see one class of the community grow immensely rich at the expense of another, to me allways [*sic*] argue'd an inefficiency in the Laws of this or any Country where it happens. If, as Goldsmith says we are hasting to the rottenness of refinement, and if such things cannot be avoided, I see no just reason for starving and condemning the laborers of the Vinyard, or keeping from them such degrees of information as they may be capable of receiving."[12] Stephen Duck, the "Thresher poet," began his writing from a point of view not unlike Bloomfield's, arguing for the dignity of rural laborers. Unfortunately, Duck himself succumbed to the social revisions that accompanied enclosure. The authentic voice of rural labor faded from his verse when he became a tour guide in the landscape garden William Kent designed for Queen Caroline, and the artificial conventions of pastoral verse replaced his accurate rural images.[13] Prolabor opinions were not limited to minor rural poets, of course. Capel Lofft defended the rights of gleaners in the Court of

Common Pleas in 1788, while Crabbe, Clare, and Wordsworth all attacked the farmers who yielded to the new, false sensibility.[14] The forces for enclosure, however, reasoned that greater production would benefit all, including the rural labor force who would have little to distract them from their loyalty to the employer.[15]

It was to a countryside changed by the dual forces of agrarian innovation and enclosure that Bloomfield returned. The changes that he had observed, sensed, and feared were accomplished facts. It was not that the rural laborer was gone or that the land was completely changed, but that the relationship in which one stood to the other was altered. If in returning to the country Bloomfield wanted to renew his place to stand (as Pope found a "place to stand, an angle of vision" in his garden and grotto)[16] Shefford did not provide it. The significant shift from present tense in his works to 1811, to the mixed tenses in *Banks of the Wye*, and finally to the past tense of *May Day with the Muses* might be a coincidental matter and not a purposeful manipulation. A similar confusion of tenses in the poetry of John Clare seems to come from viewing a scene before and after the physical changes caused by enclosure.[17] A man who has the quiet, carefully gathered, and lovingly held kind of knowledge that Bloomfield demonstrates in *The Farmer's Boy*, might instinctively change his tenses because he sensed yet another piece of knowledge: the meteoric course of his popularity and the physical and social changes in the countryside could conspire to inform the poet that his audience had not been moved by his arguments. A different kind of man, such a writer as Pope, might succeed in continuing the argument. Bloomfield could only see and sense and know that while the figurative standing place from which he argued might remain, the literal common ground on which he based his argument was gone.

The English countryside, of course, still exists, and there are prospects into which one might expect Giles to trudge. Changes that did alter the quality of rural life did not keep nature from being the material of great images in later poetry. Those same changes have not prevented the recent revival of interest in the rural poetry of such men as Clare and Bowles. But, while Bloomfield's works retained some popularity throughout the nineteenth century, the urgency they once had for their large audience is gone, and it may be that Bloomfield's major themes no longer strike us as the real or the possible. If they do not, our culture has lost something of value.

II *Bloomfield's Place in the Traditions: Pastoral and Rural Poetry*

Even if the economic possibility of the rural life Bloomfield portrayed is lost, we have not lost his record of it or his ideas of its values. As one of the earliest and best known of the nineteenth century's peasant poets, Bloomfield offers the means of identifying something of the nature of rural poetry and of both relating it to and distinguishing it from pastoral poetry. Because it is only from Bloomfield that this discussion proceeds and because other sometimes superior artists have written distinctively rural poetry, these observations can only be an explorative statement.

Hazlitt has offered one of the most important of all critical statements about Bloomfield. These early observations that place Bloomfield in "the same class of excellence" as Thomson and Cowper provide a place to begin the identification of rural poetry:

As a painter of simple natural scenery, and of the still life of the country, few writers have more undeniable and unassuming pretension than the ingenious and self-taught poet. Among the sketches of this sort I would mention, as equally distinguished for delicacy, faithfulness, and *naivete*, his description of lambs racing, of the pigs going out acorning, of the boy sent to feed his sheep before the break of day in winter; and I might add the innocently told story of the poor bird-boy, who in vain through the live-long day expects his promised companions at his hut, to share his feast of roasted sloes with him, as an example of that humble pathos, in which this author excels. The fault indeed of his genius is that it is too humble: his Muse has something not only rustic, but menial in her aspect. He seems afraid of elevating nature, lest she would be ashamed of him. Bloomfield very beautifully describes the lambs in springtime as racing round the hillocks of green turf: Thomson in describing the same image, makes the mound of earth the remains of an old Roman encampment. Bloomfield never gets beyond his own experience; and that is somewhat confined. He gives the simple appearance of nature, but he gives it naked, shivering, and unclothed with the drapery of a moral imagination. His poetry has much the effect of the first approach of spring, "while yet the year is unconfirmed," where a few tender buds venture forth here and there, but are chilled by the early frosts and nipping breath of poverty.[18]

Although I would follow neither Hazlitt's chastisement of Bloomfield's humility nor his selection of these particular, sentimental scenes, the accuracy of his observation is marked. To the list of Bloomfield's best subjects (natural scenery and "still life" of the country) should be added the full portraits of rural folk that emerge in Bloomfield's later works. Departing again from Hazlitt who sees no "moral imagination" in Bloomfield, I would argue the existence of what is indeed moral imagination—the moral conviction of value with which Bloomfield portrays his subjects.

When Hazlitt speaks of Bloomfield's limitations, and speaks rightly of the poet's acceptance of them, the limitations appear at first to be a handicap of the first order, but in analyzing *The Farmer's Boy*, the positive possibilities of those limitations have been shown. The real service that Hazlitt performs comes when he pauses to reflect on the failure of natural genius without education to produce a new and striking literature. His two possible explanations have meaning in terms of Bloomfield and rural poetry itself:

> And one reason appears to be, that though such persons, from whom we might at first expect a restoration of the good old times of poetry, are not encumbered and enfeebled by the trammels of custom, and the dull weight of other men's ideas; yet they are oppressed by the consciousness of a want of the common advantages which others have; are looking at the tinsel finery of the age, while they neglect the rich unexplored mine in their own breasts; and instead of setting an example for the world to follow, spend their lives in aping, or in despair of aping, the hackneyed accomplishments of their inferiors.[19]

When Bloomfield did "ape" with his style or with sentiment and incident borrowed from Goldsmith or Cowper, it was most unfortunate. But he handled his conservative meter well enough and made of it, at times, something distinctively his own, and borrowed sentiments and incidents were frequently transformed by his experience and art. The best of his poetry does come from his own breast, and does, as *The Farmer's Boy* clearly demonstrates, set a moral and ethical (if not stylistic) model for the world to follow. Bloomfield's poetry is distinctively rural in its subjects and ethics, and at its best imitates the orders and forms of rural life rather than other poetry.

Hazlett's second observation is more seriously a criticism of the society of readers than of writers like Bloomfield:

> Another cause may be, that original genius alone is not sufficient to produce the highest excellence, without a corresponding state of manners, passions, and religious belief: that no single mind can move in direct opposition to the vast machine of the world around it, that the poet can do

no more than stamp the mind of his age upon his works; and that all that the ambition of the highest genius can hope to arrive at, after the lapse of one or two generations, is the perfection of that more refined and effeminate style of studied elegance and adventitious ornament, which is the result, not of nature, but of art. In fact, no other style of poetry has succeeded, or seems likely to succeed, in the present day. The public taste hangs like a millstone around the neck of all original genius that does not conform to established and exclusive models. The writer is not only without popular sympathy, but without a rich and varied mass of materials for his mind to work upon and assimilate unconsciously to itself; his attempts at originality are looked upon as affectation, and in the end, degenerate into it from the natural spirit of contradiction, and the constant uneasy sense of disappointment and undeserved ridicule.[20]

Bloomfield, by accepting his limitations and celebrating rural life, wrote poetry that was soon in direct opposition to the "vast machine of the world around it." Because rural poetry as a rule accepts the limitations of the poet and his subject, it may always be in opposition to the world around it. If Bloomfield's audience was first moved by his limited argument in *The Farmer's Boy,* however, it may have been because they sympathized with his plea for the natural order. It is possible that the public sympathy against enclosure was fed by his argument and that the sympathy in turn made his work popular. His audience, too, would even have been in part composed of folk themselves displaced from the farms and villages. For a brief atypical moment, then, Bloomfield and his rural concerns might not have been in opposition to the spirit of the world.

His audience, however, could turn to other writers and other themes as its own concerns and life grew further removed from the natural order. Bloomfield with his vision of the ordered, natural, and knowable life could not well abandon those concerns which he thought gave life its meaning. It was inevitable, then, that he suffer "undeserved ridicule" and "the constant uneasy sense of disappointment" if he wished to remain a rural poet; however, his worst verse was written when he succumbed to the dangers of becoming "literary" and imitative. All of this is certainly not to say that rural poetry must be unpopular to be authentically rural, but it does suggest that rural poetry moves in partial opposition to the dominant urban concerns and to the urban demands for variety that would violate its natural limitations, and that Bloomfield's reputation may well have been in part a victim of that opposition.

Returning more specifically to what may be learned of rural

poetry from Bloomfield, we find a more positive statement about limitations by Unwin. While discussing Bloomfield he observes, "A peasant-poet is usually a humble man writing well within the orbit of his equally humble capacities. He is restricted in range, but not in excellence."[21] Of Hazlitt's observation that the poet's muse was menial in her aspect Unwin writes, "This is not a condemnation so long as prosaism is avoided, and Bloomfield generally succeeded in retaining a thoroughly plain, but poetic style."[22] The writer of rural poetry, then, is an authentically rural man, and as such is frequently of humble station, learning, and ambition, who has chosen to write of the subjects he knows. Accepting the limitations of his capacities and subjects, the rural poet makes his poetry from the stuff of rural life—the things, the people, and the affectations of the countryside. William Empson's distinctions between proletarian literature, ballads and fairy stories, and the pastoral may be of some help. The folk literature, he asserts, is "by the people, for the people, and about the people," while most fairy stories and ballads are "by" and "for" but not "about" people. The pastoral is "about" but neither "by" nor "for" the people.[23] By extension, rural poetry is certainly "about" rural people and life, and it is "by" rural people. But while it is "for" rural people, I would count it very poor rural poetry if it were *only* for rural folk.

The rural poet such as Bloomfield is not restricted to a certain set of figures, to the use of specific verse forms, or to a particular meter, but is free to use those devices which he can best manage and which best suit his subject. Again, the limitations are those of the poet himself. That the couplet and versions of the ballad dominate Bloomfield's work should not dispel the reader's expectations of meeting a preponderance of blank verse in the canon of another rural poet. If there is too little help here in deducing something of the nature of rural poetry, a brief examination of the method of the genre may be more fruitful.

Bloomfield's poetry does exhibit the delicacy, faithfulness, and naiveté that Hazlitt observed, and if I may appropriate the second term, faithfulness, to apply to his method, it may be helpful. To say simply that he attempted a faithful portrayal of rural life is to escape at once a cluster of weighty and sometimes ambiguous critical terms and an overly literal notion of any one-to-one relationship between the things of the countryside and the representation of it in his poetry. There is no promise that because Bloomfield described a cow in Suffolk his readers could be assured of finding said cow and tugging it firmly by the teat. The faithfulness is to the real spirit of the country and to the poet's experience of it. There is a freedom, then, for the poet to treat the things of nature with gentleness or harshness, to idealize or criticize the folk of the country, or to write as mythmaker or verist all without violating the idea of faithfulness or losing his concern with the real things of the country.

Rural poets with their limited range must, as part of their method, deal carefully with the problem of finding a common ground to be shared with their audience. Bloomfield was not so unlearned as to be unaware of literary traditions, but it was not in them that he sought his common ground. He did not set about writing pastoral verse to which his readers could come with expectations of meeting certain conventions—conventions that, whether followed or varied for effect, lie outside the poet. Instead, he chose a pattern of argument in *The Farmer's Boy* that led to a common ground within the limits of the poet's experience of rural life. The method is primarily one of inviting the reader onto a ground that is first the poet's but second, that of rural men. The audience can, and did with *The Farmer's Boy,* approach with certain expectations based upon what they know of nature and the countryside and mankind. The expectations of the audience restrict somewhat the latitude of the rural poet to make the countryside too impressionistic, atypical, or surreal.

Bloomfield's primary mode, I have indicated, was celebration. The more elegiac mode of his last works is still based on the impulse to celebrate. Such an impulse on the part of the rural poet can be an indication of an ethical conviction that there is much good in the nature of rural life. The vision of that good was, for Bloomfield, a balanced one, for he does not posit the countryside as an Eden full of innocents or nature as a wholly benevolent spirit that ministers to all of man's needs. Rather, we have seen that the good lies in the relationship of rural man to nature and to his fellowman, and in the quality of rural life, and in the things of the country.

These few assertions about the nature of Bloomfield's rural poetry are amplified when the kind is seen in relation to the pastoral. Although the two share certain qualities, they are vastly different; even the history of rural verse runs counter to the tradition of the pastoral. Thomas Rosenmeyer uses the term "Hesiodic" to indicate a type of verse that is traditionally "hostile to the pastoral chant."[24]

Tibullus' distinction between real agricultural scenes of labor, sweat, and pain and what Rosenmeyer calls a "pre-agriculturalist utopia" approximates that between rural and pastoral poetry. Hesiodic writing might be suggested as the tradition into which Bloomfield and the rural poets fit:

> In its origins, with Hesiod and Aristophanes, the tradition is activist, critical, and realistic. Hesiod moralizes for the benefit of his brother Perses, not concealing the burden of the labor, yet recommending it as work dear in the eyes of the gods. He takes a downright proletarian pride in the fact that he must suffer, physically and spiritually, before he can achieve success. Aristophanes, in turn, makes scornful fun of those who do not work for a living and who do not have their feet solidly on the ground. The Hesiodic code of country living is one of discipline and foresight. The farmer does not live a random life of enjoyment and self-revelation. On the contrary, he plans and saves and reins himself tightly for the sake of future gain. The Hesiodic strain demands self-imposed regimentation. One of its prominent organizing techniques is the calendar or almanac, arranging the tasks of the farmer in accordance with the seasons and the environment. . . . The calendar is didactic, and indeed didactic poetry is one branch of Hesiodic homeliness, a fact that is borne out by the many seventeenth- and eighteenth-century works modelled on Virgil's *Georgics*. The instruction is necessary, for without the expertise imparted, the harshness of the peasant's life would be overpowering.[25]

Using the term *ponos* for both labor and pain and as an indication that the philosophical stance underlying the Hesiodic demanded "that a good life furnish evidence of effort and suffering," Rosenmeyer indicates how this impulse differs from and is basically incompatible with the pastoral. Raymond Williams, too, notes the distinction by tracing significant writing about country life "from Hesiod and the more consciously literary traditions of the pastoral from the third century B.C. landscapes of Sicily, the Greek Islands, and Egypt."[26] For a writer like Bloomfield, however, following in such a tradition could be an unconscious and unpremeditated act. As a rural poet, Bloomfield was aware of other poets whose work was similar to his own (Burns, Crabbe, and later Clare) and not deaf to the contemporary critics who inevitably related him to the pastoral tradition. But rather than identify himself as part of the pastoral tradition, Bloomfield continued to be a rural man—sometimes "the farmer's boy"—and took his poetic identity from a *personal* kinship with other rural poets. His lifelong concern with the image of Burns was a personal concern; "Brother Bard, and fellow labourer," his salutation in writing to Clare, reveals again the idea of personal kinship.

Further distinctions between the rural and the pastoral are at times matters of real difference, at times matters of degree. Rural poetry is made of the stuff of rural life and made by rural bards; the real countryside and a rural bard are not at all necessary or even usual in pastoral poetry. Both celebrate something like rural life which in rural poetry can be idealized within the confines of the possible but which, in the pastoral, need only suggest the possible and not conform to it. The traditional singing match, the love plaint, or the elegy can appear in rural poetry when it speaks of love or friendship, but the rural poet does not ground his poem in such literary conventions.

The idealizing of country life in the pastoral and in the rural differs in intent as well as in degree. Amid the voluminous critical comment on the pastoral in the eighteenth century, some of which affected those writers that Bloomfield admired, Congleton (in *Theories of Pastoral Poetry in England 1684–1798*) finds the emergence of two distinct critical approaches, both of which indicate the necessity of idealizing rural life. These schools, neoclassic and rationalistic, were by the end of the century supplanted by a romantic theory of the pastoral which in its own fashion idealized rural life.

The neoclassical school of which Pope's *A Discourse on Pastoral* seems to be the major and perhaps final eighteenth-century statement was stimulated by Rapin's *Dissertatio de Carmine Pastorali* (translated into English by Thomas Creech in his *The Idylliums of Theocritus With Rapin's Discourse of Pastorals* in 1684). The resulting English neoclassic school drew its tenets for the pastoral from the writings of the ancients, especially Virgil and the critical writings of Aristotle and Horace. These tenets are summarized neatly by the editors of the Twickenham edition of Pope's *Discourse*.

The main point on which this school agreed was that a pastoral should be an "imitation" of the action of a shepherd living in the Golden Age. From this precept stemmed certain subsequent ones: a pastoral should reflect the innocence and peace of that age and the virtues and simplicity of the shepherd who lived in it; because shepherds in this ancient past were often princes or men of affairs, the characters and language should be simple and pure rather than "clownish"; the scene should be simple and decorous, as in Virgil; the matter should reflect only the simple affairs of shepherds, that is, the loves and sorrows of a simple rural life; the fable should be simple and plain, the style neat and plain.[27]

Here the idealizing arises from the attempt to create an image of that "pre-agriculturalist utopia" or Golden Age found at the end of the path of chronological primitivism. That society of shepherd princes is not immediately in the realm of the possible, and as a cultural and literary tradition it exists in the imagination of the artist. The very creation of the image requires extensive idealizing, for the image itself is ideal. The intent is not to improve upon the nature of rural things but to create a reality in art.

Second is that school which rose from the rationalistic approach to the pastoral set forth by Fontenelle in his *Discours sur la nature de l'eglogue* (published in 1688 and translated by Motteus under the title *Of Pastorals* in 1695).[28] With a typical freedom from the authority of the ancients, Fontenelle saw the pastoral as simply "a representation of the tranquillity of rural life," a notion based on certain "psychological foundations" which, as the editors of the Twickenham text have it, holds that "the laziness of man's nature finds delight in representations of the quietness and leisure of a shepherd's life, while the passion most congenial to this laziness, love, also delights." It was also Fontenelle's contention that the pleasure of the pastoral arises from the use of "illusion," or half-truth, which "consists, in exposing to the eye only the Tranquillity of a Shepherd's Life, and in dissembling or concealing its meanness, as also in showing only its Innocence, and hiding its Miseries."[29] Even before this approach to the pastoral becomes distinctively English in the hands of Thomas Tickell and others it appears to idealize more nearly in the way that the rural poet does. The method of idealizing is the selection of scene and incident. The intent is "Illusion," however, and not a faithfulness to the spirit of rural life.

In examining Thomas Tickell's *Guardian* papers on the pastoral, Congleton observes an important development: Tickell expands on Fontenelle's explanation of the pastoral's appeal by adding something close to the natural goodness of the shepherds and the love of the natural things of the country. Most important, Tickell declares that the English countryside is a proper setting for the pastoral; the use of rural England for all save climate in the pastoral would free it from the servile following of convention.[30] This is, in essence, cultural primitivism. Although such logic would appear to move the pastoral in many ways closer to the nature of rural poetry, the point in altering the locus of the poem was to facilitate the deception of the reader who could more easily, then, believe the pastoral creation. The essence of the countryside might creep into the pastoral without becoming the subject of the poem; the conventions and spirit of the pastoral could likewise appear in the rural without being the thing that the poet celebrates.

When in substituting cultural primitivism for chronological primitivism Joseph Warton and his romantic followers had their day with the pastoral, the two kinds become so close that the pastoral, for all practical purposes, ceased to exist. While extending the rationalist's claim that the pastoral should be made of local materials and suggesting the infusion of the more realistic portrayal with emotion, the romanticists desired a particularized representation of rural scenes and activities that made no distinction between cultural and chronological primitivism. Although for some the inhabitants of the rural world still remained idealized, John Aiken and Hugh Blair moved the portrayal of the rural society within the realms of the possible. The empirical and the concrete appear, as they do in rural poetry, hand in glove with an emotional appeal to the reader much like Bloomfield's in *The Farmer's Boy*. There may be more than ironic coincidence in the fact that the very last of the eighteenth-century's commentators on the pastoral was Dr. Nathan Drake whose warm praise of Bloomfield helped establish the poet's reputation. Drake, who thought the pastoral "based on a love of external nature and a high regard for the sentiment of primitive life," suggested that if the pastoral could not be written free from the restrictions of its conventional features and subjects, it should not be written at all.[31] An audience which demanded what the romantic critics did of the pastoral would not wish pastoral poetry to be written for them, but rather rural or peasant poetry in which a country man with the most intimate and authentic knowledge of the country wrote concretely about it.

Whatever the validity of Hazlitt's theory "that the poet can do no more than stamp the mind of his age upon his works," the idea itself provides a final possibility for differentiating between pastoral and Bloomfield's rural verse. The pastoral artist, being the more "educated" and consciously literary of the two, may have the power to make the stamp of the age a "more unique," personal, and conscious impression than can the rural artist. Those literary and philosophical impulses of Bloomfield's own age and the age preceding sometimes sit atop the fabric of his verse and at other times clash discordantly with his simple rural description. He writes only in stilted terms of "Nature," repository of natural goodness, acting as a foil to "Vanity." Underneath is the perfectly true idea that when man must rely upon the forces of nature to make seeds grow, he can take little credit for the event. But the capital letters and personified forces are not really Bloomfield's. It is probable too that the pastoral artist is generally more concerned with nature and the countryside as a medium which he neutralizes, then stamps with his moral, philosophical, and aesthetic colors than he is with real trees or real cows or (God forbid) real manure. The pastoralist may avoid real nature because his age tells him that it is evil and fallen, or because its roughness contradicts his aesthetic purpose, or because a great amount of particularized description of nature, even when the scenes are carefully selected, can be, as Dr. Johnson suggests, tedious.

The rural poet differs from the pastoralist (and, I might add, the romanticist) because his first concern is the things, folk, and events of the countryside which are important in themselves. Bloomfield may celebrate the Suffolk farm because it is familiar, comforting, a place of happy memory, but we have very little of the poet consciously interposing himself between the subject and the audience as an object to be appreciated before the reader can approach the rural subject. Bloomfield may idealize nature by selecting carefully the scenes he describes, but it is not done to sterilize and asepticize nature hence producing a characterless medium to be used for a "greater" purpose. His first purpose in portraying a scene is to celebrate the things in that scene; when he manipulates the parts of a scene and shows them to best advantage, his purpose is the greater celebration of the entire farm. The preface to *Wild Flowers* may indicate that Bloomfield thought that his celebration of specific scenes might end in the celebration of "general nature," for "nature in a village is very much like nature every where else."[32] To arrive at general nature through the particular and specific requires the cooperation of a reader willing to make associations and accept grand coincidences; general nature appears in the reader's imagination and not on the rural artist's page.

III   *The Themes and Values*

The natural and man-made objects of the countryside, the country folk, and country life are the stuff of Bloomfield's poetry.

Because he valued his subject for itself—found it to be precious—he took his themes and values directly from it. No elaborate system of order is superimposed. If his themes and values have a relatedness of the parts, it is simply because they rise from the whole of the countryside.

It is quite important to know first some of the things that the land and man's relationship to it are not. The countryside is neither Eden, nor site of a new Golden Age, nor a new utopia. That it may become these things in the minds of writers who use it is obvious, especially when they use a neutralized landscape as both a medium upon which to stamp their own order and a source from which to document the authenticity of their own order by showing parallels to the events and patterns and objects of nature. We can have the illusion of Eden, the Golden Age, or the new utopia being contained in the things of the countryside and growing naturally or organically from them when the natural patterns are mixed with the conceptual patterns of the artist; it is the same illusion that occurs when an object is cathected with erotic energy and appears to contain the energy. Although, as I have indicated, the rural poet may perforce bring ideas of his culture, ideas of benevolent nature, the natural goodness of man, perhaps pantheism and large parts of the eighteenth-century creed of sentimentalism to his poetry and give the land the illusion of a particular order, his distinction as rural artist comes in discovering the order already there in the country and in man's relationship to the land.

To reiterate, the land in Bloomfield's world was a literal and figurative common ground on which men could stand. It was literal ground from which the inhabitants of the manor took their living—a thing to which almost all had rights supported by tradition and law. Bloomfield's argument against the new refinement that marked the coming of capitalism to the farm is an argument for preserving the literal common ground between men on which they could see, for one classless moment, their mutual humanity. The literal common ground could not support the inhabitants of the manor if it was used capriciously and without a thought to good husbandry. In the mutual use of the land, the little society discovered and encouraged predictable patterns of social behavior; no one should misuse the commons by fencing them for exclusive use or destroy the arable land by turning his sheep in to pasture before the crops were removed. There are innumerable expectations for others and one-self that the mutual use of the land can produce. When there are reasonable expectations about the action of others, then trust, a necessity of ordered social life, is possible. The literal common ground becomes the figurative when the trust arising from that literal situation is transferred into the greater social sphere.

Of course a return to the open-field system of agriculture remains an impossibility. Establishing a series of commons on which urban man can learn what it is reasonable to expect from his neighbor may be an impracticable bit of dreaming. But the need for trust is real in any society intending to escape the rise of something akin to a police state in which voluntary trust is replaced by political protection of the individual. The fewer the reasonable expectations a society has for the peaceful and cooperative behavior of its members, the less trust its citizens will exhibit. A common ground, either literal or figurative, however, is not a value of the past that must remain out of reach in the limited world of Robert Bloomfield. It could be moved forward out of the past and used as a principle of discourse or argument, as a possible consideration in urban planning, or as a way of looking at human relationships.

Another of Bloomfield's themes arising from the land is that of the knowable life which may be, as I suggested in chapter 2, almost unknown to urban man. There is a natural order to life in the country. The seasons turn with predictable regularity and the rural occupations follow sensibly. The use of the land is cyclic in nature—the cycles enforced by seasonal change and the agricultural principles of rotation of use. Life on Mr. Austin's farm offered Bloomfield a structured existence in which an extensive knowledge of the past and careful observation of the present made the future predictable. The natural graduation and priority of events allows, even forces, a concern with the major over the minor. When it is time to plow, one plows; when it is time to milk, one milks. Scattered concerns align themselves within the order, and as life is structured by the passing of the seasons on the land, a sense of why one labors and when one will rest is possible despite the caprices of nature. The lessons of the past prompt preparation for the future and make life knowable as it may not be in the city. The necessity of considered actions is made apparent to everyone on the farm; and although farmers have ruined their land as surely as urban dwellers have befouled their environment, at least the structure for seeing cause and effect, past and present, is readily available in rural life. Part of the value of such a knowable life is the framework it creates around man. To see oneself reacting to the major demands of life without the insistent intrusion of the minor may be a rare experience in urban life; in fact, just being able to identify the major events and demands of life and separate them from the minor is not always easy amid our machines, our mixed media, and our talk—talk that may be our way of creating an order for the minor intrusions that we cannot control.

The folk of the countryside provide Bloomfield with another theme. His characters are, as he notes in the preface to *Wild Flowers*, almost always humble people; their relationship to the things of nature, to the land, is that of labor. Rural life demands work, labor, enterprise. The fulfillment of these demands becomes, if not a matter for pride, a moral imperative. Again and again the rural artist asserts that the yeoman who has labored his full deserves the rest of moral contentment. If no other idea gives value to the life of the poor, at least there is work by which their existence can be measured and shown to be responsible. This can, under slavery, extreme poverty, or any duress, be a horrid life from which generations of people have fled. Yet to Bloomfield the life of labor is more than one that passively and mindlessly accepted toil as the lot of man. Rural enterprise and labor can be a cause of joy; the matching of the human body to the natural labor for which it is suited could be a harmonious experience.

Jacques Barzun, who thinks it doubtful that the labors of technologic man are those to which he is biologically and psychologically suited, describes the ironic plight of labor in the post-enclosure times when the factory's machine has replaced the farm's tool:

> The machine deprives man at once of bodily exertion and fatigue and the dramatic victory of work. Consequently man's feelings about himself during the greater part of his waking time are not joyful or single-minded. This is true not only of strictly mechanical work in the factory; it applies to all the tasks that aid and mirror industry. In them men do not exactly know what it is they do under the name of work. Beside the machine, which is so exact and tireless and perfect, man grows weary and careless and indifferent. He cannot compete with it and has no incentive to do aught else. Production no longer depends on him. When he is away from the machine, its work and its output seem self-sufficient, yet demanding: the organization of its functions is a monstrous set of remote relationships.[33]

Rural man, whose ordered, knowable life allowed him to see that his family and perhaps a good many others relied directly on the success of his labor on the land, would have a far different idea of self. The dignity in Bloomfield's portraits of the poor is, then, believable and understandable. It is made so by their position on the land and the fulfillment that is possible in their labor. Good husbandry and the pride man can take in it expand the range of labor and fulfillment.

A second value, therefore, is apparent in the theme of labor. Work-labor-enterprise, like the talk of the city, proffers a way of structuring the world and knowing oneself. It has been suggested that we talk in order to know more exactly what it is that we think or believe, and validate it. Both intellect and emotion are excited and exercised by the process. Work, as physical as is its process, occupies the intellect and emotions too. Barzun notes the absorption of the laborer in his enterprise:

> But the inner struggle goes on: wielding the tool is not the act of the hand alone; the whole man works the ax or chisel, the scythe, the plow, the oar. The breath-borne rhythm, the concert of eye and sinew, the changing purpose and the sight of it fulfilled, the assured play of muscle that we find again in physical sports, are sensations good in themselves and they betoken art. Above all, the absorption of the self in manual work is unique. Alert yet only half conscious, the craftsman knows bliss. [34]

Bloomfield's portraits of rural labor show the same bliss. It is not the escape to unessential tasks, to the minor, that Dr. Johnson describes when he speaks of Sober repairing his coal-box or amusing himself with chemistry to pass the time painlessly and avoid the major tasks, [35] although I suspect that the city tinkerer at times indulges in an imitation of labor in an attempt to satisfy the same human needs as are satisfied by work. The best of rural labor reinforces man's perception of himself, allows man to know and feel his personal harmony with the natural order, and structures his world by allowing him to select and conquer the major or primal matters of existence. Of course rural labor has not been and is not always so, but at its best it is far more joyous than the later labor amid the machines of the city where "a new and degraded slavery annihilate[s] the self." [36]

Bloomfield's poetry and rural poetry in general have at least recorded the experiences of labor. In such cultural records lie some of our inventive possibilities. More than just a way of remembering, this record of a way of being stands open to man's future should he care to learn from it or preserve its values. With no thought of returning everyone to the plow, we may still wish to invent our future with the possibility of real labor that shares the qualities of rural labor.

There is a third major theme in Bloomfield's poetry that grows naturally from the themes of land and labor. Valuing what he did, it is inevitable that the rural poet should react negatively to that which threatened his beliefs. Bloomfield sensed, correctly, that it was the growth of the city that threatened rural life as he knew it; his antiurban stance is a result. I have demonstrated that Bloomfield's reaction was not a mindless fear of all change. He simply opposed those changes which seemed to produce less new good than the old good they destroyed. To the rural man, the city may always seem to be a perverse creation, because it has not, traditionally, fitted itself into the natural order. The smoke and fumes, the unnatural haste, the disappearance of recognizable priorities, the thoughtless waste and destruction, the impersonality and harshness, and the unnatural demands on the countryside all convinced him that the city was somehow evil. There are, of course, other, more positive ways of viewing the city, but from the vantage point of rural man, the negative is overwhelming.

Something of the same antiurban spirit appears in the pastoral and in eighteenth-century satire, too. In much of Bloomfield's poetry, the force of commentary arises from what he chooses to see in both the country and the city. When the positive qualities of the country are viewed beside the negative features of the city, the arrangement of the material is inherently critical of the latter. (The arrangement is not black and white, for he does recognize poverty and other negative features of country life.) The general picture of the country in *The Farmer's Boy*, for example, is positive. When the city is considered at all, it appears as a structural and spiritual intrusion into rural life. The only image in Bloomfield's picture of the city that gives it any order at all is that of the whirlpool, ungoverned and ungovernable. What Bloomfield found most objectionable (and probably still would were he alive) are those things which result from poorly considered action by urban people—perhaps from actions that are not considered at all. Even in Bloomfield's day, the smoke of the city hung about it a full five miles into the country. Something about the effect of the city on our minds allowed the situation to worsen for over one hundred years before any concerned and effective action was taken. If life and labor within the natural order once taught the value and necessity of considered actions, then Bloomfield and his fellow laborers have been forgotten too soon.

It is perhaps the nature of humans to forget our past, our roots, as soon as they are no longer immediately accessible to us. It is, therefore, the foolish assumption of any generation that its age is unique. Witness our constant narrow references to "today's society" or "this modern world"—evidence that we have little contact with our own past. Had the rural folk of Bloomfield's time been isolated from their own past and the heritage of their culture, they would have continued in the most primitive fashions of husbandry. Life within the natural order, a respect for labor, and a sense of responsible purpose arising from a relationship to the land—all of these encouraged a consideration of the past not as a time to return to, but as a repository of possibilities for the present and future. Bloomfield and his poetry are not of great importance to the history of humans and their letters. Still, he had a quiet vision of rural values and wisdom that is not without meaning and possibility in a technologic age, and to ignore him and his concerns is foolish. Bloomfield's artistry was marred at times by unrefined technique, but as Edmund Blunden has recently written, "few poets could equal his sensitivity towards the meaner things in Nature."[37] It is precisely that sensitivity that man must cultivate anew if he is to continue to survive within the natural order.

Notes and References

Preface

1. Edmund Blunden, *Votive Tablets* (1931; reprint ed. Freeport, N.Y.: Books for Libraries Press, 1967), p. 1.

Chapter One

1. It was probably Bloomfield's father, George, who changed the family name from Blomfield to Bloomfield. See W. H. Hart, F.S.A., ed., "Pedigree of Bloomfield," in *Selections From the Correspondence of Robert Bloomfield, The Suffolk Poet* (London: Spottiswood, 1870), p. ii.

2. William Wickett and Nicholas Duval, *The Farmer's Boy: The Story of a Suffolk Poet, Robert Bloomfield, his life and poems 1766–1823* (Lavenham, Suffolk: Terence Dalton, 1971), p. 9.

3. Edward W. Grayley, "A Memoir of the Poet's Life," *Views in Suffolk, Norfolk, and Northhamptonshire; Illustrative of the Works of Robert Bloomfield*, ed. J.[ames] Storer and J.[ohn] Greig (London: Vernor, Hood, and Sharpe, 1806), p. 38.

4. Ibid., p. 10.

5. W. White, *History, Gazetteer, and Directory of Suffolk* (Sheffield: White, 1844), p. 689.

6. Ibid., p. 690.

7. George Bloomfield, as quoted by Capel Lofft, ed., *The Farmer's Boy: A Rural Poem*, 9th ed. (London: Vernor, Hood, and Sharpe, 1806); hereafter this edition cited in the text as *L*.

8. British Library Additional, MS. 28,266, Robert Bloomfield, "Poems etc.," fol. 114 (manuscript version of proposed preface of stereotype edition of the works, 1808); hereafter cited in the text as MS 28,266, followed by the folio number. Bloomfield's poetry and prose is so full of regional and personal idiosyncracies of grammar and spelling that *sic* is where possible forsaken.

9. Robert Bloomfield, "Shooter's Hill," in *Wild Flowers; or, Pastoral and Local Poetry* (London: Vernor, Hood, and Sharpe, 1806), p. 79.

10. Manuscript note (leaf 10v) bound in *The Farmer's Boy*, 7th ed. (London, 1803); copy in the British Library. Later Bloomfield himself dismissed "A Village Girl": "This Song was never given correctly by my

155

Brother, and I have often wish'd that it had never been seen at all. But to set right at 38 what was written at seventeen will never do. . . ."

11. Wickett, p. 15.

12. Ibid.

13. Mr. John Dudbridge, a freeman of the city of London, tendered for Robert a bound apprenticeship which would spare the boy any legal trouble with the angry journeymen. George, who was to continue Robert's training in the trade, paid "by way of form" a five shilling premium for him when the boy accepted the indenture. Dudbridge became landlord to the brothers.

14. Rayner Unwin, *The Rural Muse: Studies in the Peasant Poetry of England* (London: Allen and Unwin, 1954), p. 90.

15. British Library Add. MS. 28,268, "Letters of Robert Bloomfield principally to members of his own family, 1788–1823," fols. 15–16. Hereafter cited in parentheses in the text as MS 28,268, followed by the folio number.

16. *The Remains of Robert Bloomfield* (London: Baldwin, Cradock, and Joy, 1824), II, 78–79. Later, Bloomfield observed: "Amongst the glory of England (her unparalleled Charitable Institutions), one more, I think, might be added. A fund to purchase beds for new married couples, under proper regulations, and with the accustomed recommendations as to character, and deserts. This heavy expense (to the poor) is a serious affair, and if not accomplished before the fruits of the marriage smile them in the face, then it (when most wanted) becomes more difficult still."

17. George Bloomfield, in *The Remains*, II, 198; see also Richard D. Altick, *The English Common Reader* (Chicago: University of Chicago Press, 1957), p. 62.

18. *Selections from the Correspondence of Robert Bloomfield, The Suffolk Poet*, ed. Hart, pp. 6ff., hereafter cited in the text as *C*.

19. Wickett, p. 30.

20. British Library Add. MS. 28,265, Robert Bloomfield, "Poems," a letter affixed to first of the manuscript.

21. The difficulties arising from having the octavos differ from the quartos combined with the negative public reaction to the notes, caused Bloomfield to draft a letter to Lofft telling him that the notes would be excluded from the entire second edition.

22. Wickett, p. 30.

23. The press account of his fortunes and the recent London gossip caused Mr. Allen, the master sealer, to ask whether the king had settled on Bloomfield an annuity of two hundred pounds per year, the kind of patronage which, if real, might have saved Bloomfield's finances from eventual collapse (Add. MS 28,268, fol. 118r).

24. "A Memoir of Robert Bloomfield," in *The Farmer's Boy; Rural Tales, Ballads, and Songs. To which are added Wild Flowers, etc.* [with an additional title page, engraved, which reads "The Poems of Robert Bloomfield"] (London: F. J. Nelson, 1835), p. xxv.

25. *Views in Suffolk, Norfolk, and Northhamptonshire,* ed. Storer and Greig, pp. 39–40.

26. See *A Catalogue of all the Valuable Books, Household Furniture, &c. to be sold at Auction, The Property of the Late Mr. R. Bloomfield, the Poet* (Biggleswade: Jackson, 1824).

27. *The Life and Correspondence of Robert Southey,* ed. Charles Cuthbert Southey (New York: Harper, 1851), p. 156.

28. Robert Southey, *The Lives and Works of the Uneducated Poets* (London: Humphrey Milford, 1925), p. 163.

29. *The Remains,* II, 49.

30. *A Catalogue of All the Valuable Books, Household Furniture, &c.,* p. 71.

31. His fear, apparently, was that after Sharpe's sale of his books to Cosby it would take time for the copyrights to revert to him. What Bloomfield wanted was to sell the half of the copyright due him that March to Longman's, a continuance of fourteen years. Although he did succeed, the sale was for an amount far below his expectations.

32. Joanna Southcott, a fanatically religious farmer's daughter, wrote doggerel prophecies and claimed supernatural powers and for a time had a considerable following.

33. Unwin, p. 108.

34. That Bloomfield's contest with the bookselling trade continued is evidenced by a letter to the Reverend Mr. Tillbrook written for the eventual information of Southey, who had once more determined to aid the impoverished poet. It set forth Bloomfield's situation and plans. First, Bloomfield owned outright one half of the copyright to everything he had written, and shared in the profits from it all. Second, his works were in the hands of Messrs. Baldwin and Company, who acted as printers and publishers and hence the underwriters of any new efforts to publish his poetry. Baldwin and Company, however, possessed "but a small share of the moiety of the whole copyright which is divided among the London booksellers; for Messrs. Longmans & Co. hold *half* of it, *viz.,* one-quarter of the whole works, without any responsibility to me or to anyone." Third, it was Bloomfield's opinion that Baldwin and Company had acted toward him with exemplary liberality. They had, in fact, agreed to reissue his whole canon by subscription, a plan of which Southey approved, and they had agreed to give over their share of the profits to the author. That plan was abandoned, however, "as probably being in the end less productive than a plain subscription of hard stuff or soft paper." Fourth and finally, Bloomfield announced that his last plan had been activated and that Southey was requested to deposit anything he could raise with a banking house in London. With some resignation he noted, "At present the sale of the poems is diminished; and I hardly know what is not diminished, except the public debt" (*C,* 60).

35. Cobbet and Hunt are men whom I would not trust with power; they are too

eager to obtain it.—Universal suffrage is an impracticable piece of nonsense [sic];—
Republicanism will only do in *New* established countrys' [sic], not in those which
have been govern'd by Kings for a thousand years.—It is the natural bent and
practice of *party* to go to extreems [sic]. Thus they could not let me rest even on the
intermediate shelf of Scepticism but made me a Deist at once!!—I have been in the
presence of great and *good* men, the Bishops Watson and Porteous, but then it is
equally true that I have taken snuff with Horne Tooke, and have held conversation
with Handy the Boatmaker, who was tried for high treason!—Yea, more than all this,
I had the misfortune to be born only six miles from the birthplace of Tom Paine!!
This, to some ears would be horrible!— — —I shall go to worship again when I am
well enough; and when my dear Daughter and Sons can leave me in company of a
Woman whom you know little about, they will go too (Add. MS 28,268, fol. 423).

With the circumstantial evidence playfully introduced, Bloomfield implied
that all the possible accusations were absurd. The woman Baker knew little
about was, of course, Bloomfield's wife whose theological affinity to Johanna
Southcott, the religious fanatic, Baker thought unfortunate.

36. Wickett, p. 62.
37. *May Day with the Muses* (London: Baldwin, Cradock, and Joy,
1822), p. viii.
38. John Tibble and Anne Tibble, *John Clare: His Life and Poetry*
(London: Heinemann, 1956), pp. 33–34.
39. British Library Egerton MS. 2245, "The MS Letters of John Clare,"
I, 1818–1821, fol. 186r–v.
40. British Library Add. MS. 30,809, "Poems and Papers of Robert
Bloomfield and His Eldest Son Charles, 1791–1825," fol. 66.
41. *The Remains*, II, 129.
42. Bloomfield had once written of children's books:

I never get hold of a child's book but I feel an inclination to see how the story is
told, be it ever so simple. If I can judge by my girls, the minds of children are much
interested by such as are well written; and it appears of much importance to have
them adapted to their years; by the exclusion of words which they cannot be
acquainted with:—and, surely, if that curse of beauty and loveliness—affectation, was
unsparingly attacked, it would have a good effect. 'Jemima Placid' is a charming thing
in this way. 'Virtue in a Cottage,' is a most pleasing and naturally told story, written
by somebody who had seen something besides the shop windows in Cheapside. I
shall remember the 'Dog's nose' in 'Goody-two-shoes,' as long as I live. My mother
read it to me and my sister, when very young, and enforced its precepts, and its
excellent hits at superstition, in a manner which I shall ever esteem the greatest for
her favours, and the most unquestionable proof of her love and her understanding. As
soon as I can find time, I mean to try my hand at some trifle for the use of
children (*Remains,* II, 120–21).

43. "Advertisement," in *Hazelwood Hall: A Village Drama* (London:
Baldwin, Cradock, Joy, 1823), pp. iii–iv.
44. Graham F. Reed, "Bloomfield's Aeolus," *Notes and Queries,* 102
(October, 1956), 450–51.

45. Wickett, p. 63.

46. *The Letters of John Clare*, ed. J.[ohn] W. and Anne Tibble (London: Routledge, 1951), p. 158.

47. *The Remains*, I, 93.

48. Ibid., II, 102.

49. British Library Add. MS. 30,809, fol. 32.

Chapter Two

1. The poem soon sold nearly thirty thousand copies, according to Rossiter Johnson, ed., *Works of the British Poets*, vol. 2 (New York: Appleton, 1876), p. 58. Five editions in the first two years, nine by 1806, and fourteen separate editions during Bloomfield's lifetime attest to the poem's popularity.

2. [Robert Southey], Review of *The Farmer's Boy: a Rural Poem*, in *The Critical Review, or Annals of Literature*, 29 (May, 1800), 66–77.

3. Review of *The Farmer's Boy; A Rural Poem*, in *The Monthly Review, or Literary Journal*, 32 (September, 1800), 50–56. (See too *The Monthly Mirror*, 9 (March, 1800), 163–66; (May, 1800), 225–28).

4. *Collected Letters of Samuel Taylor Coleridge, 1785–1800*, ed. Earl Leslie Griggs (Oxford: Clarendon Press, 1956), I, 623.

5. *Literary Hours* (London: Cadell and Davies, 1800), II, 444.

6. George Dyer, as quoted by Unwin, p. 103.

7. Dwight L. Durling, *Georgic Tradition in English Poetry* (1935; reprint ed. New York: Kennikat, 1963), p. 97.

8. Ibid., pp. 100–101.

9. Ian Jack, "Poems of John Clare's Sanity," in *Some British Romantics*, ed. James V. Logan (Columbus, 1966), pp. 223–24.

10. Robert Bloomfield, *The Farmer's Boy; A Rural Poem* 1st 8vo. ed. (London: Vernor and Hood, 1800), p. 95; hereafter cited in the text. Page numbers are offered since the line numbers are not always accurate, and the pagination remains almost constant through the editions arranged by the author.

11. Having seen the manuscript, Bloomfield returned it with a letter stating, "You are not the first who noticed the Omission of the Hay-making: the best excuse I have to offer is, that in composing the Poem I was determined that what I said on farming should be EXPERIMENTALLY true. There was on that small farm no hay to make; it formed no part of my business; and Thompson has described it most charmingly" *(An Appendix to the Season of Spring, in the Rural Poem, "The Farmer's Boy"* (Croyden, Surrey: [J. Holland?], 1806), p. 3.

12. Coleridge, II, 913. Coleridge himself makes this identification.

13. *Selections from the Correspondence of Robert Bloomfield, The Suffolk Poet*, Hart, p. 29.

14. Edmund Blunden, *Nature in English Literature* (Port Washington, New York: Kennikat, 1970), p. 120.

15. William Wordsworth, "Preface to the Second Edition of the 'Lyrical Ballads,' in *The Poetical Works,* ed. E. de Selincourt, 2d ed. (Oxford: Clarendon Press, 1952), II, 393.

16. "The Seasons," in *Poetical Works,* ed. J. Logie Robertson (London: Oxford University Press, 1965), p. 3.

17. Ibid.

18. Ibid.

19. Note that Bloomfield chooses the same adjective for gunners as for foxes. It is as if both predators are natural facts, both with their uses, and both to be accepted as part of the natural order.

20. Blunden, p. 121.

21. Ibid., p. 122.

22. Unwin, p. 98.

23. Ibid.

24. Blunden, p. 123.

25. Ibid., p. 123.

26. Ibid.

27. E. W. Bovill, *English Country Life: 1780–1830* (London: Oxford University Press, 1962), p. 231.

28. Blunden, p. 127.

29. Ibid., p. 129.

Chapter Three

1. Roland, Grant, ed., *A Selection of Poems by Robert Bloomfield* (London: Grey Wells Press, 1947), p. 14.

2. Unwin, p. 106.

3. "Bloomfield's Aeolus," *Notes and Queries,* 201 (October, 1956), 451.

4. Blunden, p. 131.

5. Unwin, p. 106.

6. Review of *Rural Tales, Ballads, and Songs,* in *The Critical Review,* 35 (May, 1802), 67–75.

7. Review of *Rural Tales, Ballads, and Songs,* in *The Monthly Mirror,* 13 (January, 1802), 24, 28.

8. *The Letters of John Clare,* p. 167.

9. *Rural Tales, Ballads, and Songs,* 1st ed. with notes by Capel Lofft (London: Vernor and Hood, 1802), p. 1; hereafter cited in the text as *R.* As line and verse numbers do not appear in each poem and are sometimes incorrectly given, page numbers will be provided.

10. Wordsworth, indeed, is sometimes incapable of fulfilling the promise of humble speech made in his poetry. In "Resolution and Independence," for example, there are five times as many lines expended in rhapsody about the old man's speech as there are lines representing it.

When those lines of dialogue finally come they are rather flat and disappointing.

11. *The Complete Works of William Hazlitt*, ed. P. P. Howe, vol. 17 (London: Dent, 1933), p. 239.

12. Claire Blunden, in a letter to the author, March 24, 1970.

13. *Wild Flowers; or Pastoral and Local Poetry* (London: Vernor, Hood, and Sharpe, 1806), p. iii; hereafter cited in the test as W.

14. Page ix, wrongly printed "xi."

15. Review of *Wild Flowers, or Pastoral and Local Poetry*, in *The Critical Review*, 3d ser. 2 (June, 1802), 123.

16. Ibid., p. 127.

17. John Barrell, *The Idea of Landscape and the Sense of Place 1730–1840: An Approach to the Poetry of John Clare* (Cambridge: Cambridge University Press, 1972). Barrell's excellent study of the pictorial background to Clare is a good source for those studying the impact of social and economic reality upon a rural poet's images. See pp. 94–97.

18. Bloomfield's note: "Box Hill, and the beautiful neighborhood of Dorking, in Surrey."

19. Robert Bloomfield, *The Banks of the Wye* (London: Vernor, Hood, and Sharpe, 1811), p. 3; hereafter cited in the text as B.

20. Barrell, pp. 98–109.

21. Unwin, p. 107.

22. *May Day with the Muses* (London: Baldwin, Cradock, and Joy, 1822), p. 3; hereafter cited in the text as M.

Chapter Four

1. Sister Mary Eulogie Horning, *Evidences of Romantic Treatment of Religious Elements in Late Eighteenth-Century Minor Poetry (1771–1800)* (Washington: Catholic University Press, 1932), p. vii.

2. *The Poetical Works of the Rev. George Crabbe: with his Letters and Journals, and his life by his son.* (London: John Murray, 1834), I, 245.

3. Unwin, p. 104.

4. John Lawrence Hammond and Barbara Hammond, *The Village Labourer: 1760–1832, A Study in the Government of England before the Reform Bill* (1913; Reprint ed. New York: A. M. Kelley, 1967), p. 27.

5. John Lawrence Hammond and Barbara Hammond, *The Rise of Modern Industry* (London: Methuen, 1966), p. 85.

6. Bovill, p. 13.

7. Hammond, *The Rise of Modern Industry*, p. 84.

8. Bovill, p. 13.

9. As quoted in ibid., p. 14.

10. Hammond, *The Rise of Modern Industry*, p. 88.

11. British Library Add. MS. 28,268, "Letters of Robert Bloomfield principally to members of his own family, 1788–1823," fol. 111.

12. Ibid., fol. 96.

13. Raymond Williams, *The Country and the City* (New York: Oxford University Press, 1973), pp. 88–89.

14. Kenneth MacLean, *Agrarian Age: A Background for Wordsworth* (New Haven: Yale University Press, 1950), pp. 60–61.

15. Hammond, *The Rise of Modern Industry*, p. 89.

16. Maynard Mack, *The Garden and the City: Retirement and Politics in the Later Poetry of Pope, 1731–1743* (Toronto: University of Toronto Press, 1969), p. 32.

17. Barrell, pp. 96–97, 110–20.

18. "On Thomson and Cowper," in *The Complete Works of William Hazlitt*, V, 95–96.

19. Ibid., p. 96.

20. Ibid.

21. Unwin, p. 95.

22. Ibid.

23. William Empson, *Some Versions of Pastoral* (Norfolk, Conn.: New Directions, 1950), p. 6.

24. Thomas G. Rosenmeyer, *The Green Cabinet: Theocritus and the European Pastoral Lyric* (Berkeley: University of California Press, 1969), p. 20.

25. Ibid., p. 21.

26. Williams, p. 14.

27. E. Audra and Aubrey Williams, eds., *Pastoral Poetry and an Essay on Criticism*, by Alexander Pope, vol. 1 (New Haven: Yale University Press, 1961), p. 15.

28. Ibid., p. 16.

29. Ibid.

30. J. E. Congleton, *Theories of Pastoral Poetry in England: 1684–1798* (Gainesville: University of Florida Press, 1952), pp. 87–88.

31. Ibid., p. 144.

32. Robert Bloomfield, *Wild Flowers; or Pastoral and Local Poetry* (London: Vernor, Hood, & Sharpe, 1806), p. viii.

33. Jacques Barzun, *Science: The Glorious Entertainment* (New York: Harper & Row, 1964), pp. 34–35.

34. Ibid., p. 32.

35. *The Idler and The Adventurer*, ed. W. J. Bate, John M. Bullitt, and L. F. Powell, vol. 2 (New Haven: Yale University Press, 1963), pp. 97–98.

36. Barzun, p. 34.

37. Edmund Blunden, in a written statement to the author, March 24, 1970.

Selected Bibliography

PRIMARY SOURCES

1. Manuscripts.
Bloomfield's unpublished correspondence and the notes and prefaces in the handwritten volumes of poetry are the major sources for the biography as it is presented in this study.
"Letter to John Clare, 1820." British Library Egerton Manuscript 2245, fol. 186.
"Original Letters of Robert Bloomfield principally to members of his own family, 1788–32." British Library Additional Manuscript 28, 268.
"Poems and Papers of Robert Bloomfield and His Eldest Son Charles, 1791–1825." British Library Additional Manuscript 30, 809.
"Poems, etc." British Library Additional Manuscript 28,266.
"Poems: May Day with the Muses; The Banks of the Wye; etc." British Library Additional Manuscript 26, 265.

2. Published Materials.
Bloomfield's popularity was such that his works are readily available in their original editions in research libraries. The second item is typical of several fascimile editions in which those without access to a large library are apt to encounter him. Listed here are the first editions and subsequent editions which are of bibliographical and biographical interest.
The Banks of the Wye; A Poem. London: Vernor, Hood, and Sharpe; Longman, Hurst, Reese, Orme and Brown, 1811.
Collected Poems (1800–1822). Intro. Jonathan N. Lawson. Gainesville, Florida: Scholars' Facsimiles and Reprints, 1971.
"Extract from a Poem, entitled 'Good Tidings, or News from the Farm,' by Robert Bloomfield. Recited at the Anniversary Meeting of the Royal Jennerian Society, Thursday, 17th of May, 1804." London: James Whiting, 1804.
The Farmer's Boy; A Rural Poem. 1st 8vo. ed. London: Vernor and Hood, 1800.
The Farmer's Boy; A Rural Poem. 7th ed. Manuscript notes by the author. London: Vernor and Hood; Longman and Rees, 1803. The edition is in the British Library.

The Farmer's Boy; A Rural Poem. 9th ed. London: Vernor, Hood, and
    Sharpe; Longman, Hurst, Rees, and Orme, 1806.
Hazelwood Hall: A Village Drama. London: Baldwin, Cradock, and Joy,
    1823.
The History of Little Davy's New Hat. London: Harvey and Darton, 1815.
May Day with the Muses. London: The Author; Baldwin, Cradock, and Joy,
    1822.
The Remains of Robert Bloomfield. Edited by Joseph Weston. 2 vols.
    London: Baldwin, Cradock, and Joy, 1824. Includes much material
    between boards for the first time.
Rural Tales, Ballads and Songs. 3d ed. With notes by Capel Lofft. London:
    Vernor and Hood, Longman and Rees, 1802.
A Selection from the Poems of Robert Bloomfield. Edited by J. L. Carr with
    a foreword by Edmund Blunden. Kettering: J. L. Carr, 1966. The
    preface is a facsimile of Mr. Blunden's handwriting.
A Selection of Poems by Robert Bloomfield. Edited by Roland Gant.
    London: Grey Wells Press, 1947. Part of the Crown Classics series; has
    an interesting and sympathetic preface.
*Selections from the Correspondence of Robert Bloomfield, The Suffolk
    Poet.* Edited by W. H. Hart, F.S.A. London: Spottiswoode, 1870. A
    facsimile edition by Robert Ashby (Redhill, Surrey: Commercial
    Lithographic Company, 1969) is also available.
Wild Flowers; or, Pastoral and Local Poetry. 1st sm. 8vo. ed. London:
    Vernor, Hood, and Sharpe; Longman, Hurst, Rees, and Orme, 1806.
*A Catalogue of all the Valuable Books, Household Furniture, &c. To be
    Sold by Auction, by W. Betts, on Friday & Saturday, the 28th & 29th
    of May, 1824, The Property of the Late Mr. R. Bloomfield, The Poet,
    on the Premises, at Shefford, Beds.* Biggleswade: Jackson, 1824. Final
    notes to the biography of the poet can be found among the physical
    remains of his estate.

SECONDARY SOURCES

1. Biographical.

Capel Lofft's preface and notes in the various early editions of *The Farmer's
    Boy* form the basis of most of the following biographies. For particulars
    on Lofft see his life as communicated by himself to the *Monthly
    Mirror,* 13 (June, 1802), 370–76; 14 (July, 1802), 9–14.
"A." "A Memoir of Robert Bloomfield." in *The Poetical Works of Robert
    Bloomfield and Henry Kirke White.* London: T. Nelson, 1871. This
    reworking of previous facts and opinions shows considerable sympathy
    for Bloomfield still existing in the second half of the century.
A Biographical Sketch of Robert Bloomfield, with a Portrait. N.p. [1825].
    Copy in the British Library. A typical and highly derivative biography.
EVANS, JOHN. Letter to the Editors. *Metropolitan Literary Journal,* 3

(1823–1824), 424–29. Comments on some matters of biography previously discussed in the journal.

G. V. L. "A Biographical Sketch of Robert Bloomfield." *Monthly Mirror*, 10 (October, 1800), 202–5. One of the first major public notices of interest in Bloomfield.

HOLLAND, JOSEPH. *An Appendix to the Season of Spring in the Rural Poem, "The Farmer's Boy."* Croyden, Surrey: [Joseph Holland?], 1806. An interesting footnote to the career of Bloomfield.

"On the Life and Writings of Robert Bloomfield." *Metropolitan Literary Journal*, 3 (1823–1824), 208–17. See too "Additions and Corrections to the Article, "On the Life and Writings, etc.,"" pp. 326–27 for Bloomfield's obituary notice.

RANDS, WILLIAM B., ed. *The Poetical Works of Robert Bloomfield: A New Edition with A Sketch of the Author's Life and Writings.* London: Knight, 1855. Also of interest for its description of Bloomfield's reputation by mid-century.

STORER, J[AMES], and GREIG, J[OHN], eds. *Views in Suffolk, Norfolk, and Northamptonshire; Illustrative of the Works of Robert Bloomfield; Accompanied with Descriptions: To which is Annexed, A Memoir of the Poet's Life, by Edward Wedlake Brayley.* London: Vernor, Hood, and Sharpe, 1806. Includes an interesting account by Bloomfield.

WICKETT, WILLIAM, and DUVAL, NICHOLAS. *The Farmer's Boy: The Story of a Suffolk Poet, Robert Bloomfield, His Life and Poems, 1766–1823.* Lavenham, Suffolk: Terence Dalton, 1971. Of more value for its biographical information than its criticism.

2. Critical and Biographical.

BLUNDEN, EDMUND. *Nature in English Literature.* 1929; reprint ed., New York: Kennikat Press, 1970. Helpful chapter on Bloomfield. Contains a valuable chapter on Bloomfield and *The Farmer's Boy*.

HAZLITT, WILLIAM. "On Thomson and Cowper." In *The Complete Works of William Hazlitt*, edited by P. P. Howe, V, 95ff. London: Dent, 1930. Balanced and insightful remarks on Bloomfield.

REED, GRAHAM F. "Bloomfield's Aeolus." *Notes and Queries*, 201 (October, 1956), 450–51. A generally unsympathetic view.

SOUTHEY, ROBERT. *The Lives and Works of the Uneducated Poets.* London: Humphrey Milford, 1925. Sympathetic remarks by one of Bloomfield's most generous champions.

3. Major Contemporary Reviews.

For nearly fifteen years dozens of small, sometimes borrowed reviews of Bloomfield appeared in such publications as the *Lady's Monthly Museum*, attesting not only to his general popularity but also to his specific appeal to women. A lengthy listing of contemporary reviews is available in William S. Ward's *Literary Reviews in British Periodicals:*

1789–1820 (New York: Garland, 1972). See especially reviews in the *Monthly Review*, the *Monthly Mirror*, and the *Critical Review*.

4. Background Materials and General Criticism.

AUBIN, ROBERT ARNOLD. *Topographical Poetry in XVIII–Century England.* 1936; reprint ed., New York: Kraus, 1966. Study of a tradition into which much of Bloomfield's work falls.

AUDRA, E., and WILLIAMS, AUBREY, eds. *The Poems of Alexander Pope.* Vol. 1. *Pastoral Poetry and an Essay on Criticism.* New Haven: Yale University Press, 1961. Provides a useful history of the eighteenth-century pastoral.

BARRELL, JOHN. *The Idea of Landscape and the Sense of Place 1730–1840: An Approach to the Poetry of John Clare.* Cambridge: Cambridge University Press, 1972. A provocative study of the relationship of landscape painting to the poetry of the period, especially as the poetry reflects the social and economic facts of country life.

BARZUN, JACQUES. *Science: The Glorious Entertainment.* New York: Harper & Row, 1964. A fascinating examination of modern values and attitudes which in many cases are antithetical to Bloomfield's.

BISHIP, MORCHARD, ed. *Recollections of the Table-Talk of Samuel Rogers.* London: Richards Press, 1952. Bloomfield's sometimes friend and patron, Samuel Rogers, provides a full picture of the successful side of the London literary scene—a side Bloomfield only glimpsed, and then, in part, through Rogers.

BLUNDEN, EDMUND. "The Rural Tradition." In *Edmund Blunden: A Selection of His Poetry and Prose.* London: Rupert Hart-Davis, 1950. A helpful essay which details something of the history and motivation of the poetic protest against enclosure and which identifies some of the values held by the writers in the tradition.

BOVILL, E. W. *English Country Life: 1780–1830.* London: Oxford University Press, 1962. A full discussion of the background against which Bloomfield lived and wrote.

CLARE, JOHN. *The Letters of John Clare.* Edited by J[ohn] W. Tibble and Anne Tibble. London: Routledge, 1945. Of value here for numerous references to and praise of Bloomfield.

COLERIDGE, SAMUEL TAYLOR. *Collected Letters of Samuel Taylor Coleridge.* Edited by Earl Leslie Griggs. 4 vols. Oxford: Clarendon Press, 1956. Noted here for their reference to Bloomfield.

CONGLETON, J. E. *Theories of Pastoral Poetry in England: 1684–1798.* Gainesville: University of Florida Press, 1952. The neoclassic and rationalistic schools of the pastoral are thoroughly examined.

CRABBE, GEORGE. *The Poetical Works of the Rev. George Crabbe: with His Letters and Journals and His Life.* 8 vols. London: John Murray, 1834. Bloomfield's more successful contemporary deals with many of the same images and situations, but does so more successfully and more sternly.

DURLING, DWIGHT L. *Georgic Tradition in English Poetry*. 1935; reprinted., New York: Kennikat, 1963. Helpful background to pastoral and rural verse.

EMPSON, WILLIAM. *Some Versions of Pastoral*. Norfolk, Conn.: New Directions, 1950. An examination of what the pastoral is and is not which traces the spirit of the pastoral into modern poetry and novels.

HAMMOND, JOHN LAWRENCE, and HAMMOND, BARBARA. *The Rise of Modern Industry*. 1926; reprint ed., London: Methuen, 1966. The effects of industry on English country life are followed and interpreted by the authors. Their studies of the laboring classes are useful background for understanding Bloomfield in his element.

————. *The Skilled Labourer: 1760–1832*. 1936; reprint ed., New York: A. M. Kelley, 1967.

————. *The Town Labourer: 1760–1832*. *The New Civilization*. 1941; reprint ed., New York: A. M. Kelley, 1967.

————. *The Village Labourer: 1760–1832*. *A Study in the Government of England before the Reform Bill*. 1913; reprint ed., New York: A. M. Kelley, 1967.

JACK, IAN. "Poems of John Clare's Sanity." In *Some British Romantics: A Collection of Essays*. Edited by James V. Logan et al. Ohio State University Press, 1966. Reveals some of Clare's debt to Bloomfield with little sympathy for the latter.

JOHNSON, ROSSITER. *Works of the British Poets, from Chaucer to Morris with Biographical Sketches*. Vol. 2. *Rogers to Hermans*. New York: Appleton, 1876. Of interest chiefly for its prefaces dealing with such minor figures as Bloomfield.

KERMODE, FRANK, ed. *English Pastoral Poetry: From the Beginnings to Marvell*. Toronto: George C. Harrap, 1952. The introduction of value for its overview of the kind.

MACLEAN, KENNETH. *Agrarian Age: A Background for Wordsworth*. New Haven, Yale Studies in English, vol. 15. New Haven: Yale University Press, 1950. Describes in detail what is also the background for Bloomfield.

ROSENMEYER, THOMAS G. *The Green Cabinet: Theocritus and the European Pastoral Lyric*. Berkeley: University of California Press, 1969. Identifies fully the roots of the tradition of rural poetry.

SOUTHEY, ROBERT. *The Life and Correspondence of Robert Southey*. Edited by Charles Cuthburt Southey. New York: Harper, 1851. Of interest here for its chronicling of Southey's patronage of Bloomfield.

THOMSON, JAMES. *Poetical Works*. Edited by J. Logie Robertson. London: Oxford University Press, 1956. Bloomfield's chief literary source for *The Farmer's Boy*.

TIBBLE, JOHN, and TIBBLE, ANNE. *John Clare: His Life and Poetry*.

London: Heinemann, 1956. Provides valuable critical background while discussing Bloomfield's "Brother Bard."

Tributary Verses to the Memory of Robert Bloomfield, The Suffolk Poet. Woodbridge, England, 1823. Some evidence is here of the limited notice that marked Bloomfield's death.

UNWIN, RAYNER. *The Rural Muse: Studies in the Peasant Poetry of England.* London: Allen and Unwin, 1954. Perhaps the best serious examination of the tradition in which Bloomfield really belongs. A generally sympathetic yet objective study.

WILLIAMS, RAYMOND. *The Country and the City.* New York: Oxford University Press, 1973. A major modern study of two metaphors that were of great importance to Bloomfield. Williams' insistent Marxism flavors his reading of such minor figures as Cuck, Clare, and Bloomfield.

WHITE, W. *History, Gazetteer, and Directory of Suffolk.* Sheffield: White, 1844. Of interest for its picture of early nineteenth-century Suffolk and for its references to Bloomfield, Lofft, and Grafton.

WORDSWORTH, WILLIAM. *The Poetical Works.* Edited by E. de Selincourt. 2d ed. 5 vols. Oxford: Clarendon Press, 1952. One can hardly read Bloomfield properly without setting him against the considerable and contrasting shadow of Wordsworth across this period.

Index

Aiken, John, 147
Aristotle, 145
Austin, William, 14–16, 19, 26, 37, 57, 136, 150

Baker, Thomas Lloyd, 36, 44–46; Mrs., 37, 38, 39
Baldwin, Cradock and Joy (publishers), 43–44, 50
Bancroft, Joseph, 32
Bantock, Nancy (early sweetheart), 19
Barbauld, Ann Laetitia, 28, 32
Barton, Bernard, 32
Barzun, Jacques, 151–52
Bent, W. (*Universal Magazine*), 21
Bewick, Thomas, 136
Blair, Hugh, 147
Bloomfield, Charles (son), 23, 30, 41, 47, 48, 50, 110
Bloomfield, Charlotte (daughter), 41
Bloomfield, George (brother), 13–20, 22, 24, 25, 26, 29, 43, 49
Bloomfield, George (father), 13, 122, 155nl
Bloomfield, Hannah (daughter), 20, 30, 37, 39, 41, 42, 44, 51, 52
Bloomfield, Mary Anne Church (wife), 20, 21, 23, 41
Bloomfield, Nathaniel (brother), 24, 34, 40
Bloomfield, Robert, adult reading, 32; Aeolian harps, 20, 28, 32, 35, 52; appointed to seal office, 29; arrival in London, 15; birth, 13; death, 51; early learning, 14, 16–18; early poems, 17; farmwork, 14; legal apprenticeship, 18–19; literary life an annoyance, 23, 25–26, 32, 35–36; love of the commons or green, 13, 82, 137; marriage, 20; prodigious memory, 24, 28–29; rumors of

radicalism, 44–46; shoemaking, 16–19, 25, 26; struggles to support family, 23, 29–31, 40–43, 48, 50–51; subscription by patrons, 42–43; tour of the Wye, 35–38, 120

WORKS—EARLY PIECES:
"Sailor's Return, The," 17
"Village Girl, A," 17, 155n10

WORKS—GENERAL:
Banks of the Wye, 35, 40, 49, 138; analysis of, 123–25; composition of, 36–38; critical reception, 37
Farmer's Boy, The, 18, 25–27, 30, 32, 40, 94–95, 97, 99–100, 105–106, 109–11, 114, 118, 120, 122, 135–38, 140–41, 143, 147, 153; antiurban themes in, 60, 62, 71–72, 77, 82, 88; Composition of, 20–23; idealization in, 59, 91; patron for, 22–24; pattern of argument in, 59–63, 67, 69–70, 72–75, 79–82, 88, 91–92; pictorialism in, 69–70; reviews of, 54–55; rural values in, 57, 66–68, 70–71, 75–77, 79, 82–83, 85–86, 88, 90–91; setting of, 56–58; speakers voice in, 61–62, 65, 67, 71, 73, 82, 84–85, 92; structure of, 56–63, 79, 89–90, 92
Hazelwood Hall: A Village Drama, 48–50, 63
History of Little Davy's New Hat, The, 35, 42, 48–49
May Day with the Muses, 40, 53, 138; composition of, 43–46; critical reception of, 46; return to rural themes in, 126, 128; sent to John Clare, 47; speaker's voice in, 126, 131